Conversations with F. Scott Fitzgerald

Literary Conversations Series

Peggy Whitman Prenshaw
General Editor

Photo credit: Bruccoli Collection of F. Scott Fitzgerald, Thomas
Cooper Library, University of South Carolina

Conversations
with F. Scott Fitzgerald

Edited by
Matthew J. Bruccoli and Judith S. Baughman

University Press of Mississippi
Jackson

www.upress.state.ms.us

The University Press of Mississippi is a member of the Association of American University Presses.

Copyright © 2004 by University Press of Mississippi
Manufactured in the United States of America

11   10   09   08   07   06   05   04   03   4   3   2   1
∞
Library of Congress Cataloging-in-Publication Data

Fitzgerald, F. Scott (Francis Scott), 1896–1940.
    Conversations with F. Scott Fitzgerald / edited by Matthew J.
  Bruccoli and Judith S. Baughman.
       p.   cm.—(Literary conversations series)
    Includes bibliographical references and index.
    ISBN 1-57806-604-2 (alk. paper)—ISBN 1-57806-605-0 (pbk. : alk.
  paper)
       1. Fitzgerald, F. Scott (Francis Scott), 1896–1940—Interviews.   2.
  Authors, American—20th century—Interviews.   3. Fiction—Authorship.   I.
  Bruccoli, Matthew Joseph, 1931–   II. Baughman, Judith.   III. Title.   IV.
  Series.
  PS3511.I9Z463   2004
  813'.52—dc21   2003010741

British Library Cataloging-in-Publication Data available

Books by F. Scott Fitzgerald

Fie! Fie! Fi-Fi! Cincinnati, New York, and London: The John Church Co., 1914. 17 song lyrics. *Fie! Fie! Fi-Fi! A Facsimile of the 1914 Acting Script and the Musical Score,* introduction by Matthew J. Bruccoli. Columbia: University of South Carolina Press for the Thomas Cooper Library, 1996.

The Evil Eye. Cincinnati, New York, and London: The John Church Co., 1915. 17 song lyrics.

Safety First. Cincinnati, New York, and London: The John Church Co., 1916. 21 song lyrics.

This Side of Paradise. New York: Scribners, 1920; London: Collins, 1921. Novel.

Flappers and Philosophers. New York: Scribners, 1920; London: Collins, 1922. Stories.

The Beautiful and Damned. New York: Scribners, 1922; London: Collins,1922. Novel.

Tales of the Jazz Age. New York: Scribners, 1922; London: Collins, 1923. Stories.

The Vegetable. New York: Scribners, 1923. Play.

The Great Gatsby. New York: Scribners, 1925; London: Chatto and Windus, 1926. Novel. *The Great Gatsby: A Facsimile of the Manuscript,* ed. Bruccoli. Washington: Bruccoli Clark/ NCR, 1973. Cambridge Edition, ed. Bruccoli. Cambridge and New York: Cambridge University Press, 1991.

All the Sad Young Men. New York: Scribners, 1926. Stories.

Tender Is the Night. New York: Scribners, 1934; London: Chatto and Windus, 1934. Novel. *Tender Is the Night, "With the Author's Final Revisions,"* ed. Malcolm Cowley. New York: Scribners, 1951; London: Grey Walls, 1953. Facsimile annotated by Bruccoli. London: Samuel Johnson, 1995. Everyman Centennial Edition, ed. Bruccoli. London: Everyman/ Dent, 1996.

Taps at Reveille. New York: Scribners, 1935. Stories.

The Last Tycoon. New York: Scribners, 1941; London: Grey Walls, 1949. Unfinished novel. With *The Great Gatsby* and 5 stories. *The Love of the Last Tycoon: A Western,* Cambridge Edition, ed. Bruccoli. Cambridge and New York: Cambridge University Press, 1993.

The Crack-Up, ed. Edmund Wilson. New York: New Directions, 1945. Essays, selections from *Notebooks,* and letters.

The Stories of F. Scott Fitzgerald, ed. Cowley. New York: Scribners, 1951.

Afternoon of an Author, ed. Arthur Mizener. Princeton, N.J.: Princeton University Library, 1957; New York: Scribners, 1958; London: Bodley Head, 1958. Stories and essays.

The Pat Hobby Stories, ed. Arnold Gingrich. New York: Scribners, 1962; Harmondsworth: Penguin, 1967.

The Letters of F. Scott Fitzgerald, ed. Andrew Turnbull. New York: Scribners, 1964; London: Bodley Head, 1964.

The Apprentice Fiction of F. Scott Fitzgerald, ed. John Kuehl. New Brunswick, N.J.: Rutgers University Press, 1965.

Thoughtbook of Francis Scott Key Fitzgerald, ed. Kuehl. Princeton, N.J.: Princeton University Library, 1965.

Dearly Beloved. Iowa City, Iowa: Windhover Press, 1970. Story.

F. Scott Fitzgerald in His Own Time: A Miscellany, ed. Bruccoli and Jackson R. Bryer. Kent, Ohio: Kent State University Press, 1971. Poems and lyrics, contributions to *The Princeton*

Tiger and *The Nassau Literary Magazine,* reviews, letters, articles, and interviews. Also material about Fitzgerald.

Dear Scott/Dear Max: The Fitzgerald-Perkins Correspondence, ed. Kuehl and Bryer. New York: Scribners, 1971; London: Cassell, 1973.

As Ever, Scott Fitz——: Letters Between F. Scott Fitzgerald and His Literary Agent Harold Ober 1919–1940, ed. Bruccoli and Jennifer M. Atkinson. Philadelphia and New York: J. B. Lippincott, 1972; London: Woburn, 1973.

The Basil and Josephine Stories, ed. Bryer and Kuehl. New York: Scribners, 1973.

F. Scott Fitzgerald's Ledger (A Facsimile), ed. Bruccoli. Washington: Bruccoli Clark/NCR, 1973.

Bits of Paradise, ed. Bruccoli and Scottie Fitzgerald Smith. London: Bodley Head, 1973; New York: Scribners, 1974. Stories, including 10 stories by Zelda Fitzgerald.

Preface to This Side of Paradise. Iowa City, Iowa; Windhover Press, 1975.

The Cruise of the Rolling Junk. Bloomfield Hills, Mich. and Columbia, S.C.: Bruccoli Clark, 1976. 3 travel articles.

F. Scott Fitzgerald's Screenplay for Eric Maria Remarque's Three Comrades, ed. Bruccoli. Carbondale and Edwardsville: Southern Illinois University Press, 1978.

The Notebooks of F. Scott Fitzgerald, ed. Bruccoli. New York and London: Harcourt Brace Jovanovich/Bruccoli Clark, 1978.

F. Scott Fitzgerald's St. Paul Plays, ed. Alan Margolies. Princeton, N.J.: Princeton University Library, 1978.

The Price Was High, ed. Bruccoli. New York and London: Harcourt Brace Jovanovich/Bruccoli Clark, 1979; London: Quartet, 1979. Stories.

Correspondence of F. Scott Fitzgerald, ed. Bruccoli and Margaret M. Duggan, with Susan Walker. New York: Random House, 1980.

Poems 1911–1940, ed. Bruccoli, with intro. by James Dickey. Bloomfield Hills, Mich. and Columbia, S.C.: Bruccoli Clark, 1981.

F. Scott Fitzgerald: Inscriptions. Columbia, S.C.: Matthew J. Bruccoli, 1988.

The Short Stories of F. Scott Fitzgerald, ed. Bruccoli. New York: Scribners, 1989; London: Scribners, 1991.

Babylon Revisited: The Screenplay, intro. by Budd Schulberg. New York: Carroll and Graf, 1993.

F. Scott Fitzgerald: A Life in Letters, ed. Bruccoli with the assistance of Judith S. Baughman. New York: Scribners, 1994.

F. Scott Fitzgerald on Authorship, ed. Bruccoli with Baughman. Columbia: University of South Carolina Press, 1996. Reviews, essays, interviews, public statements, and excerpts from *Notebooks.*

F. Scott Fitzgerald: The Princeton Years: Selected Writings, 1914–1920, ed. Chip Deffaa. Fort Bragg, Calif.: Cypress House Press, 1966.

Trimalchio: A Facsimile Edition of the Original Galley Proofs for The Great Gatsby, afterword by Bruccoli. Columbia: University of South Carolina Press in Cooperation with the Thomas Cooper Library, 2000.

Before Gatsby: The First Twenty-Six Stories, ed. Bruccoli with the assistance of Baughman. Columbia: University of South Carolina Press, 2001.

Facsimile Collection

F. Scott Fitzgerald Manuscripts, ed. Matthew J. Bruccoli. New York and London: Garland, 1990–1991. 18 vols.: *This Side of Paradise, The Beautiful and Damned, The Great Gatsby* galleys, *Tender Is the Night, The Love of the Last Tycoon, The Vegetable,* stories, and articles.

Biographical/Bibliographical Studies

Matthew J. Bruccoli, *Some Sort of Epic Grandeur: The Life of F. Scott Fitzgerald,* Second Revised Edition (Columbia: University of South Carolina Press, 2002)

Bruccoli, *F. Scott Fitzgerald: A Descriptive Bibliography,* Revised Edition (Pittsburgh: University of Pittsburgh Press, 1987)

Scottie Fitzgerald Smith, Bruccoli, and Joan P. Kerr, *The Romantic Egoists* (New York: Scribners, 1974; Columbia: University of South Carolina Press, 2004)

Another one for Scottie

Contents

Introduction

This volume prints thirty-seven interviews with F. Scott Fitzgerald. Most of them are not standard interviews but instead reports that quote the writer, the journalistic custom in the twenties. The only extended Fitzgerald interview is the 1922 three-parter by Thomas Boyd in the *St. Paul Daily News.*

Fitzgerald died before the authorial interview became a literary subgenre after World War II. George Plimpton and the *Paris Review* were largely responsible for the development of the intensive, writer-at-work interview commencing in 1953.[1] The enabling factor in transforming the authorial interview into literary history was probably the availability of portable tape recorders in the fifties. We have in-depth interviews with William Faulkner and Ernest Hemingway who lived through this era, but not with Thomas Wolfe or Theodore Dreiser, who died earlier.

Fitzgerald enjoyed his celebrity, but he had a poor sense of public relations and provided interviewers with opportunities to trivialize him. He didn't know the rules: Never trust a reporter, and never indulge in irony when talking to a reporter. Hemingway, who knew the rules, was treated respectfully in the press; Fitzgerald was usually treated condescendingly. Seven of his interviews—five printed before 1924—have *flapper* in their headlines. John O'Hara, the soundest Fitzgerald authority among his contemporaries, commented on the promiscuous application of the term *flapper* to Fitzgerald's women:

> From the literary point of view, one of the worst things that ever happened to
> Fitzgerald was the simultaneous popularity of John Held's drawings. Those
> damn editorial writers were largely to blame. Who would want to take Fitzger-
> ald seriously if all they ever knew about him was that he wrote about those John
> Held girls? Held was a very good satirist, and he didn't *want* his girls to be
> taken seriously. Of course Fitzgerald was partly to blame. He called one book
> *Flappers and Philosophers,* and in the public mind the flapper was the John
> Held girl. Actually, of course, Fitzgerald and Held and the editorial writers were
> all misusing the word *flapper.* A flapper was English slang, and it meant a
> society girl who had made her debut and hadn't found a husband. On the shelf,
> they used to say. It wasn't an eighteen-year-old girl with flopping galoshes.[2]

In the twenties Fitzgerald was regarded as a spokesman for rebellious youth, as a playboy, as an authority on sex and marriage, as an expert on Prohibition, as a sensational popular writer. He was not regarded as one of the best American writers who ever lived or as the author of one of the greatest novels in the English language. Although envy may have motivated some of the reporters, Fitzgerald was not the victim of outright malice—except from the reprehensible Michel Mok, who humiliated a sick man. Then, as now, reporters wanted a good story and were more interested in gossip than in literary values.

The twenties have been cheapened by the media as an era of irresponsibility and dissipation. Fitzgerald, who became a totemic figure of the Jazz Age—which he claimed credit for naming—has been trivialized by people who attend parties in silly clothing and dance the Charleston incompetently. The truth is that more major American writers functioned during the twenties than at any other time: Hemingway, Wolfe, Lardner, Cozzens, O'Neill, H. L. Mencken, Hammett, Cather, Faulkner, Dreiser, Pound, Eliot, Frost. . . . It was the second and greater American Renaissance in all the arts, but literature had special value. The twenties were the last time in American life when writers were heroes. Yet Fitzgerald got a bad press. The reporters—along with many newspaper book-reviewers—declined to accord him the respect they granted to his contemporaries. One of the reasons was his popularity as a *Saturday Evening Post* writer, which did not carry over to the sales of his novels: *The Great Gatsby* sold fewer than 23,870 copies in 1925. The opinion-makers were unable or unwilling to recognize that Fitzgerald's stories and novels provided the same stylistic brilliance. Again John O'Hara: "Fitzgerald was a better just plain writer than all of us put together. Just words writing."

These reports are worth salvaging because they document the state of Fitzgerald's public image and literary reputation during his decade of early success and the following decade of discouragement. The evidence provided by the interviews assists literary historians to understand the extraordinary posthumous Fitzgerald revival. Renewed interest in Fitzgerald began as the post–World War II period looked to an earlier postwar period for possible models of behavior. The newspaper image of Fitzgerald inherited from the twenties and thirties provided a figure who appealed to general readers and to non-reading groupies but ultimately brought new and more serious readers to F. Scott Fitzgerald as well. The revival commenced in 1945, five years after Fitzgerald's death, with the publication of *The Crack-Up*, edited by Edmund

Wilson; *The Portable F. Scott Fitzgerald,* edited by Dorothy Parker with John O'Hara's strong introduction; the Armed Services Edition of *The Great Gatsby,* distributed gratis during World War II; and the first mass-market paperback of *The Great Gatsby,* Bantam #8, which sold for twenty-five cents. Unlike most literary revivals—those of Henry James and Herman Melville, for example—the Fitzgerald revival was generated by readers, not academics. In 1951 the first full-length biography appeared, and by the 1960s Fitzgerald was firmly placed among the major American writers.

In accordance with the University Press of Mississippi's Literary Conversations series style, factual blunders in the interviews have been retained but are corrected in the notes. Obvious typographical errors have been silently corrected.

MJB

JSB

Notes

1. Harvey Breit began publishing short interviews with writers in the *New York Times Book Review* in 1948.

2. "Mrs. Stratton of Oak Knoll," *Assembly* (New York: Random House, 1961), p. 19.

Chronology

1896   24 September: Birth of Francis Scott Key Fitzgerald to Edward and Mary ("Mollie") McQuillan Fitzgerald at 481 Laurel Avenue, St. Paul.

1898   April: After failure of his St. Paul furniture factory, Edward Fitzgerald takes job as salesman with Procter & Gamble in Buffalo, New York; until July 1908, the Fitzgerald family resides in Buffalo or Syracuse.

1900   24 July: Birth of Zelda Sayre to Anthony and Minnie Machen Sayre in Montgomery, Alabama.

1908   March: Edward Fitzgerald loses his job, and in July the Fitzgerald family returns to St. Paul. FSF enters St. Paul Academy in September.

1911   August: FSF's first play, *The Girl from Lazy J,* is produced in St. Paul. September: FSF enters Newman School, Hackensack, New Jersey.

1912   August: Production of FSF's second play, *The Captured Shadow,* in St. Paul.

1913   August: Production of FSF's third play, *"Coward,"* in St. Paul. September: FSF enters Princeton University with class of 1917; meets Edmund Wilson '16 and John Peale Bishop '17.

1914   September: Production of FSF's fourth play, *Assorted Spirits,* in St. Paul. Fall: FSF first contributes to the *Princeton Tiger.* December: Production of *Fie! Fie! Fi-Fi!,* FSF's first Princeton Triangle Club show.

1915   April: FSF begins publishing in the *Nassau Literary Magazine.* 28 November: FSF drops out of Princeton for remainder of junior year. December: Production by Triangle Club of *The Evil Eye,* for which FSF wrote lyrics.

1916   September: FSF returns to Princeton as member of Class of 1918. December: Production by the Triangle Club of *Safety First,* for which FSF wrote lyrics.

1917   26 October: FSF receives commission as infantry 2nd lieutenant. 20 November: FSF reports to Fort Leavenworth, Kansas; begins novel "The Romantic Egotist."

1918   End of February: FSF completes first draft of "The Romantic Egotist" on leave at Princeton; submits novel to Scribners. March–June: FSF receives military training at army camps in Kentucky, Georgia, and Montgomery, Alabama. July: FSF and Zelda Sayre meet at country club dance in Montgomery. August: Scribners declines "The Romantic Egotist"; revised typescript rejected in October. November: War ends before FSF's unit is sent overseas.

1919   February: FSF is discharged from army. Planning to marry Zelda Sayre, he goes to New York, works for the Barron Collier advertising agency, and tries unsuccessfully to break into the magazine market. June: Zelda Sayre breaks engagement. July–August: FSF quits advertising job and returns to St. Paul; rewrites novel while living with parents. 16 September: Maxwell Perkins of Scribners accepts novel, now titled *This Side of Paradise*. November: FSF becomes client of literary agent Harold Ober.

1920   Mid-January: Engagement to Zelda Sayre resumes during FSF's visits to Montgomery. 21 February: Becomes *Saturday Evening Post* author with "Head and Shoulders." 26 March: Publication of *This Side of Paradise*. 3 April: Marriage of FSF and Zelda Sayre at rectory of St. Patrick's Cathedral in New York. 10 September: Publication of *Flappers and Philosophers*, FSF's first short story collection.

1921   August (until October 1922): Fitzgeralds rent homes in and near St. Paul. 26 October: Birth of the Fitzgeralds' daughter, Scottie.

1922   4 March: Publication of *The Beautiful and Damned*. 22 September: Publication of *Tales of the Jazz Age*, FSF's second collection of short stories. Mid-October (until April 1924): Fitzgeralds rent house at 6 Gateway Drive in Great Neck, Long Island. Friendship with Ring Lardner.

1923   27 April: Publication of FSF's play *The Vegetable*, which fails at its Atlantic City tryout in November.

1924   May: Fitzgeralds move to France; settle in June at Villa Marie, Valescure, St. Raphaël. Summer–Fall: FSF completes *The Great Gatsby*. October (until February 1925): Fitzgeralds are in Rome, where FSF revises galleys of *The Great Gatsby*.

1925   10 April: Publication of *The Great Gatsby*. Late April: Fitzgeralds move to Paris. May: FSF meets Ernest Hemingway in Paris. Summer: FSF plans early version of Tender Is the Night.

1926   February: Play version of *The Great Gatsby*, by Owen Davis, produced on Broadway. 26 February: Publication of *All the Sad Young Men*, FSF's third short story collection. Early March: Fitzgeralds return to Riviera; live at Juan-les-Pins. December: Fitzgeralds return to America.

1927   January: Fitzgeralds go to Hollywood where FSF works on screenplay (not produced) for United Artists; meets actress Lois Moran and producer Irving Thalberg. March (until March 1928): Fitzgeralds rent "Ellerslie," near Wilmington, Delaware. ZF begins ballet lessons.

1928   April: Fitzgeralds return to Europe; rent apartment at 58 rue de Vaugirard, Paris. Mid-summer: ZF begins ballet training with Mme. Lubov Egorova in Paris. 7 October: Fitzgeralds return to "Ellerslie."

1929   March: Fitzgeralds return to Paris and the Riviera, where, in June, they rent Villa Fleur des Bois, Cannes.

1930   23 April–11 May: Suffering her first emotional breakdown, ZF is hospitalized at Malmaison Clinic outside Paris. 22 May: ZF is hospitalized at Val-Mont Clinic in Glion, Switzerland. 5 June: ZF enters Prangins Clinic at Nyon, Switzerland. Summer and Fall: FSF lives in Switzerland.

1931   15 September: ZF released from Prangins. Fitzgeralds return to America. September (until Spring 1932): Fitzgeralds rent house in Montgomery. FSF goes to Hollywood alone to work on *Red-Headed Woman* for Metro-Goldwyn-Mayer.

1932   12 February: 1932 ZF suffers second breakdown; enters Phipps Psychiatric Clinic of Johns Hopkins Hospital in Baltimore. March: ZF completes first draft of her novel, *Save Me the Waltz,* while at Phipps Clinic. 20 May (until November 1933): FSF rents "La Paix" at Towson outside Baltimore. 26 June: ZF discharged from Phipps; joins family at "La Paix." 7 October: Publication of ZF's novel, *Save Me the Waltz.*

1933   December: FSF rents house at 1307 Park Avenue, Baltimore.

1934   12 February: ZF's third breakdown; returns to Phipps Clinic. 12 April: Publication of *Tender Is the Night.* 19 May: ZF transferred to Sheppard-Pratt Hospital outside Baltimore.

1935   February: FSF at Oak Hall Hotel in Tryon, North Carolina. 20 March: Publication of *Taps at Reveille,* FSF's fourth short story collection. Summer: FSF at Grove Park Inn, Asheville, North Carolina. September: FSF in Baltimore. November: FSF in Hendersonville, North Carolina.

1936   February–April: "The Crack-Up" essays published in *Esquire.* 8 April: ZF enters Highland Hospital in Asheville. July (until June 1937): FSF lives at Grove Park Inn, then at Oak Hall Hotel in Tryon, North Carolina.

1937   July: Deeply in debt, FSF goes to Hollywood for third time with six-month MGM contract at $1,000 a week. On 14 July meets movie columnist Sheilah Graham, who becomes his companion. July (until

February 1938): FSF works on *Three Comrades* script, his only
screen credit. December: FSF's MGM contract is renewed for one
year at $1,250 a week.

1938 February (until January 1939): FSF works on unproduced scripts for
"Infidelity," *Marie Antoinette, The Women,* and *Madame Curie.* December: FSF's MGM contract is not renewed.

1939 10–12 February: FSF travels to Dartmouth College with Budd
Schulberg to work on *Winter Carnival;* fired for drunkenness. March
(until October 1940): FSF takes freelance jobs at Paramount, Universal, Twentieth Century-Fox, Goldwyn, and Columbia studios. Summer: FSF begins work on *The Love of the Last Tycoon.*

1940 ca. 15 April: ZF discharged from Highland Hospital; lives with her
mother in Montgomery but returns to Asheville when unwell. 21 December: FSF dies of heart attack at Sheilah Graham's Hollywood
apartment. 27 December: FSF buried in Rockville Union Cemetery,
Rockville, Maryland.

1941 27 October: Publication of *The Last Tycoon,* edited by Edmund
Wilson.

1945 12 August: Publication of *The Crack-Up,* edited by Wilson.

1948 10 March: ZF dies in fire at Highland Hospital. 17 March: ZF buried
with FSF.

1975 7 November: FSF and ZF reinterred in the Fitzgerald family plot at
St. Mary's church, Rockville, Maryland.

Conversations with F. Scott Fitzgerald

Books

Heywood Broun / 1920

Reprinted from the *New York Tribune,* 7 May 1920, p. 14.[1]

Having from time to time set down our impressions of F. Scott Fitzgerald, who wrote *This Side of Paradise,* it seems only fair to step aside and let Mr. Fitzgerald talk for himself, as he does in an interview by Carleton R. Davis, which is sent to us by Scribner's.

"With the distinct intention of taking Mr. Fitzgerald by surprise I ascended to the twenty-fifth floor of the Biltmore[2] and knocked in the best waiter-manner at the door. On entering, my first impression was one of confusion—a sort of rummage sale confusion. A young man was standing in the center of the room, twining an absent glance first at one side of the room and then at the other.

"'I'm looking for my hat,' he said, dazedly. 'How do you do? Come on in and sit down on the bed.'

"The author of *This Side of Paradise* is sturdy, broad shouldered and just about medium height. He has blond hair, with the suggestion of a wave, and alert green eyes—mélange somewhat Nordic—and good looking, too, which was disconcerting, as I had somehow expected a thin nose and spectacles.

"We had preliminaries—but I will omit the preliminaries—they consisted in searching for things, cigarettes, a blue tie with white dots, an ash tray. But as he was obviously quite willing to talk and seemed quite receptive to my questions, we launched off directly on his ideas of literature.

"'How long did it take to write your book?' I began.

"'To write it—three months. To conceive it—three minutes. To collect the data in it—all my life. The idea of writing it occurred to me on the first of last July. It was sort of a substitute form of dissipation.'[3]

---

[1] Shortly after the publication of *This Side of Paradise,* Fitzgerald wrote a self-interview to be used in publicizing his book. The Scribners book-advertising manager, John William Rogers, did not print the interview but some forty years later allowed *Saturday Review* to publish it in the magazine's 5 November 1960 issue. Parts of the interview did appear in "The Author's Apology," a glossy sheet signed by Fitzgerald and tipped into copies of the third printing of *This Side of Paradise* distributed at a May 1920 meeting of the American Booksellers Association.

[2] The Biltmore Hotel in Manhattan, where the Fitzgeralds honeymooned.

[3] Enforcement of Prohibition began on 1 July 1919.

"'What are your plans now?' I asked him.

"He gave a long sigh and shrugged his shoulders.

"'I'll be darned if I know. The scope and depth and breadth of my writings lie in the laps of the gods. If knowledge comes naturally, through interest, as Shaw learned his political economy or as Wells devoured modern science— why, that'll be slick. On study itself—that is, in 'reading up' a subject—I haven't anthill moving faith. Knowledge must cry out to be known—cry out that only I can know it, and then I'll swim in it to satiety, as I've swum in—in many things.'

"'Please be frank.'

"'Well, you know if you've read my book, I've swum in various seas of adolescent egotism. But what I meant was that if big things never grip me— well, it simply means I'm not cut out to be big. This conscious struggle to find bigness outside, to substitute bigness of theme for bigness of perception, to create an objective *Magnum Opus* such as "The Ring and the Book"[4]— well, all that's the antithesis of my literary aims.

"'Another thing,' he continued. 'My idea is always to reach my generation. The wise writer, I think, writes for the youth of his own generation, the critics of the next and the schoolmasters of ever afterward.[5] Granted the ability to improve what he imitates in the way of style, to choose from his own interpretation of the experiences around him what constitutes material, and we get the first-water genius.'

"'Do you expect to be—to be—well, part of the great literary tradition?' I asked, timidly.

"He became excited. He smiled radiantly. I saw he had an answer to this.

"'There's no great literary tradition,' he burst out. 'There's only the tradition of the eventual death of every literary tradition. The wise literary son kills his own father.'

"After this he began enthusiastically on style.

"'By style, I mean color,' he said. 'I want to be able to do anything with words: handle slashing, flaming descriptions like Wells, and use the paradox with the clarity of Samuel Butler, the breadth of Bernard Shaw and the wit of Oscar Wilde. I want to do the wide sultry heavens of Conrad, the rolled-gold sundowns and crazy-quilt skies of Hichens[6] and Kipling, as well as the

[4] Robert Browning's long poem published in 1868–1869.
[5] Fitzgerald used this statement—and the one about the gestations and composition of the novel—in "The Author's Apology."
[6] English novelist Robert Hichens, who was known for his lush style.

pastel dawns and twilights of Chesterton.[7] All that is by way of example. As a matter of fact, I am a professed literary thief, hot after the best methods of every writer in my generation.'"

Having heard Mr. Fitzgerald, we are not entirely minded to abandon our notion that he is a rather complacent, somewhat pretentious and altogether self-conscious young man.[8]

---

[7] English novelist and man of letters G. K. Chesterton.

[8] An influential reviewer, Broun did not like *This Side of Paradise*, though he later gave *The Great Gatsby* a favorable review.

Fitzgerald, Flappers and Fame

Frederick James Smith / 1921

Reprinted from *Shadowland*, 3 (January 1921), 39, 75.

F. Scott Fitzgerald is the recognized spokesman of the younger generation—the dancing, flirting, frivoling, lightly philosophizing young America—since the publication of his now famous flapper tale, *This Side of Paradise*. Perhaps our elders were surprised to discover, as Mr. Fitzgerald relates, that the young folk, particularly the so-called gentler sex, were observing religion and morals slightly flippantly, that they had their own views on ethics, that they said damn and gotta and whatta and 'sall, that older viewpoints bored them and that they both smoked cigarets and admitted they were "just full of the devil."

All of which *is* the younger generation as Fitzgerald sees it. Indeed, the blond and youthful Fitzgerald, still in his twenties, is of, and a part of, it. He left Princeton in the class of '17 and, like certain young America, slipped into the world war *via* the training camp and an officership. We suspect he did it, much as the questioning hero of *This Side of Paradise*, because "it was the thing to do." He was a lieutenant in the 45th Infantry and later an aide to Brigadier General Ryan. It was in training camp that he first drafted *This Side of Paradise*.

"We all knew, of course, we were going to be killed," relates Fitzgerald with a smile, "and I, like everybody else, wanted to leave something for posterity." But the war ended and Fitzgerald tried writing advertising with a New York commercial firm. All the time he was endeavoring to write short stories and sell them, but every effort came back with a rejection slip. Finally, Fitzgerald resolved upon a desperate step. He would go back to his home in St. Paul and live a year with his parents, aiming consistently to "get over."

Then he sold his first story to *Smart Set* in June 1918, receiving thirty dollars therefrom.[1] He worked for three months rewriting *This Side of Paradise*—and sold it to Scribner's. Success came with a bang and now Fitzgerald is contributing to most of the leading magazines. At the present moment he is completing his second novel, to be ready shortly.

---

[1] "Babes in the Woods," which was published in the September 1919 *Smart Set*, was revised from a 1917 *Nassau Literary Magazine* story.

"I realize that *This Side of Paradise* was immature and callow, just as such critics as H. L. Mencken and others have said, altho they were kind enough to say I had possibilities. My new novel will, I hope, be more mature. It will be the story of two young married folk and it will show their gradual disintegration—broadly speaking, how they go to the devil. I have one ideal—to write honestly, as I see it.

"Of course, I know the sort of young folks I depict *are* as I paint them. I'm sick of the sexless animals writers have been giving us. I am tired, too, of hearing that the world war broke down the moral barriers of the younger generation. Indeed, except for leaving its touch of destruction here and there, I do not think the war left any real lasting effect. Why, it is almost forgotten right now.

"The younger generation has been changing all thru the last twenty years. The war had little or nothing to do with it. I put the change up to literature. Our skepticism or cynicism, if you wish to call it that, or, if you are older, our callow flippancy, is due to the way H. G. Wells and other intellectual leaders have been thinking and reflecting life. Our generation has grown up upon their work. So college-bred young people, here and in England, have made radical departures from the Victorian era.

"Girls, for instance, have found the accent shifted from chemical purity to breadth of viewpoint, intellectual charm, and piquant cleverness. It is natural that they want to be interesting. And there is one fact that the younger generation could not overlook. All, or nearly all, the famous men and women of history—the kind who left a lasting mark—were, let us say, of broad moral views. Our generation has absorbed all this. Thus it is that we find the young woman of 1920 flirting, kissing, viewing life lightly, saying damn without a blush, playing along the danger line in an immature way—a sort of mental baby vamp. It is quite the same with the boys. They want to be like the interesting chaps they read about. Yes, I put it all up to the intellectuals like Wells.

"Personally, I prefer this sort of girl. Indeed, I married the heroine of my stories. I would not be interested in any other sort of woman."

We asked Fitzgerald about motion pictures. "I used to try scenarios in the old days," he laughed. "Invariably they came back. Now, however, I am being adapted to the screen. I suspect it must be difficult to mold my stuff into the conventional movie form with its creaky mid-Victorian sugar. Personally, when I go to the pictures, I like to see a pleasant flapper like Constance Talmadge, or I want to see comedies like those of Chaplin's or Lloyd's. I'm not strong for the uplift stuff. It simply isn't life to me."

Scott Fitzgerald Here on Vacation; "Rests" by Outlining New Novels

Thomas Alexander Boyd / 1921

Reprinted from the *St. Paul Daily News,* 28 August 1921, p. E6.

Mandarin-like, slow, but with a decided accent very hard on the heels was the descent of F. Scott Fitzgerald from the authorish and presumably supernal regions of the house which he is inhabiting at Dellwood, White Bear Lake.

A pair of pajamas, robin's egg blue, carefully and tightly girded in at the waist; above the jacket a smooth straight neck supported a face that the girls would call terribly beautiful.

The agreeable countenance of a young person who cheerfully regards himself as the center of everything, Scott Fitzgerald is not unlike Amory Blaine, the romantic egotist. His eyes are blue and domineering; nose is Grecian and pleasantly snippy; mouth, "spoiled and alluring" like one of his own yellow-haired heroines; and he parts his wavy fair hair in the middle, as Amory Blaine decided that all "slickers" should do.

Mr. and Mrs. Fitzgerald have taken the home of Mackey Thompson at Dellwood for three months. They have just returned from a short visit to Europe. Fitzgerald is hard at work on some short stories which will be published in popular magazines. He has three new novels planned, he says.

We talked about books and contemporary authors. H. L. Mencken, the Baltimore critic, reminds him of a red-faced, good-natured, German beer-drinker who loves to sit around in his shirt sleeves and his stocking feet.

Here are some of the quaint sayings, fascinating facts and literary gems that fell from the Fitzgerald lips:

"Carl Sandburg came into prominence as a poet because the great city of Chicago felt the need of a representative poet, and pinned the badge on Carl because nobody else was around!"

"Floyd Dell has reached the depth of banality in his book, *Moon-Calf.*"

"Charlie Chaplin is one of the greatest men in the world. You might as well protest against a Cunarder[1] as to protest against the movies."

"The war was nothing but a natural disturbance, and is eclipsed in importance by the income tax."

---

[1] Vessel owned by the Cunard Line.

"Sherwood Anderson gets his effects in spite of his style which is very bad."

"I am looking forward to the new books this fall by Ben Hecht, John Dos Passos, and Charles Norris. The latter's novel, *Brass*, has been sent me by the *Bookman* for review."[2]

"I don't care much for Joseph Hergesheimer. My new novel is a work something like *Linda Condon*."

I was surprised to learn that Mr. Mencken was not known to Mr. Fitzgerald at the time he wrote his novel, *This Side of Paradise*. It seemed to me that Mr. Mencken's influence on both *This Side of Paradise* and on Sinclair Lewis's *Main Street*, was too obvious to be overlooked. However, Mr. Fitzgerald says that a young man at college, from whom Burne Holiday is modeled, was the greatest influence in his writing.[3]

"Hugh Walpole[4] was the man who really started me writing. One day I picked up one of his books when I was riding on a train. I thought, 'If this fellow can get away with it as an author, I can too.' His book seemed to me to be as bad as possible, but I knew they sold like hot cakes. The principal thing he did was to make unessentials seem important. I dug in after that and wrote my first novel.

"Europe made very little impression on me. I rather liked London, but France and Italy represent a decaying civilization. In Italy, the house where Keats died—a close, dismal hole which looked out on a cluttered, squalid street through which diseased children ran[5]—was to me a compendium of the affectation that people have for Italy. When Anatole France dies there will be nothing left of La Belle France."

I pray God and Mr. Fitzgerald to forgive me for inaccuracies!

Scott Fitzgerald is a youth that American literature will have to reckon with. To how great an extent depends upon himself. He has definitely shown that he can write first-rate stuff. As a literary craftsman he is admirable.

Yet, we have an odious number of literary craftsmen writing for popular magazines today. Perhaps there is no nation in the world where the technic of writing so abounds as it does in our country. But, almost to the last man, these writers tell their audience nothing new. In this strife to reach the best-seller class, contemplation so necessary to serious and lasting work is neglected. Hand-painted bowls filled with air.

---

[2] Fitzgerald's review appeared as "Poor Old Marriage," *The Bookman* (November 1921).

[3] Character in *This Side of Paradise* partly based on Henry Strater.

[4] English social novelist.

[5] The Keats-Shelley Memorial is at the Spanish Steps in Rome, which was not a slum.

Technical difficulties which must be faced by the young writer are enormous. In an attempt to master these difficulties he often loses sight of the real purpose of writing. So, we have Robert W. Chambers, fine literary craftsman, Richard Harding Davis, teller of the dashing type of short story, and a hundred others, who twenty or thirty years ago were promising young men as Scott Fitzgerald is today.

They are now frustrated artistic figures with paunches for souls.

Critics and other knowing persons have placed great hopes in Mr. Fitzgerald. At his early age he has already developed a lucid style, he has a brilliant gift for phrasing, a trick of picturization, a talent for unearthing that which lies just below the obvious.

I had the advantage of reading *This Side of Paradise* before I had ever seen any of Mr. Fitzgerald's short stories. I have no doubt he wrote the story of Amory Blaine solely to please himself. The book has a deep ring that comes from sincerity. I can imagine him chuckling gayly as he set down certain passages in it. But malice was not permitted to get the upper hand of honesty.

His short stories, almost without exception, show that there was one thing uppermost in his mind when he was writing them and that was no more nor less than $350. No thought was required to write "The Cut Glass Bowl" and "The Four Fists." These stories have been done more competently in many languages. "Head and Shoulders" and "The Offshore Pirate" are mere titillations for oafs and lumpheads. "Dalrymple Goes Wrong" was the only story in *Flappers and Philosophers* I cared for. Each short story is competently phrased.

Now Mr. Fitzgerald has written another novel, *The Beautiful and Damned*, which is being published in one of our popular gaudy magazines. After a careful perusal of the first installment I gasped. The characteristics that made Amory Blaine so attractive have been assiduously woven into his new hero's makeup. His paragraphs sparkle like well-cut, many-faceted gems, but he has not nearly sounded the depths.

However, I found the original manuscript to be much better. It will be printed by Scribner's without the deletions which mar the serial. The editors to whom the manuscript was submitted cut out every third line that was not sensational. They chopped it down from 130,000 to 90,000 words. An especially good description of Anthony Patch was torn out.[6]

---

[6] Fitzgerald sent Boyd's novel *Through the Wheat* to Scribners editor Maxwell Perkins; it was published in 1923.

Literary Libels: Francis Scott Key Fitzgerald

Thomas Alexander Boyd / 1922

Reprinted from the *St. Paul Daily News,* 5 March, 12 March, and 19 March 1922, City Life section, p. 6.

St. Paul presents to the eye the spectacle of a huge city clinging tenaciously to the east and alarmed over the danger of falling into the west. One of the remaining tentacles that saves it from falling over this ignominious brink is the pronunciation of the name; good St. Paul residents whose names are in the social register call it Sin Paul. Thus, a stranger coming to St. Paul and wishing only to know the socially elect could well be guided by the pronunciation of the town's name.

It was here that Francis Scott Key Fitzgerald was born and here that he wrote his first novel. In the interim of these two notable events he seems to have wandered afield: entering a preparatory school in the east, spending four years at Princeton, and visiting friends in Washington and New York. Then the United States entered the war and Fitzgerald made off for an officer's training camp, subsequently to become a first lieutenant. After spending more than a year at Camp Taylor, Camp Gordon, and Camp Sheridan, Alabama, Fitzgerald returned to New York where he tried to make his living writing advertisements. But he wanted to get married and he knew he could not do so on the money he was earning. So he returned to St. Paul and, in an attic room of his mother's home on Summit Ave., began to rewrite a book of which he had written the first draft in training camp. It took three months of hard work to complete the book and two weeks after it had been sent to the publishers, it was accepted. It really was the first popular young man's novel that was at all serious and as a result it brought to the Fitzgerald pockets an almost fabulous amount of money.[1] With that sum and with a fairly open market for his future brain brats he married and set up an establishment in New York.

When I came to St. Paul I was interested most in meeting people who

---

[1] *This Side of Paradise* sold about 50,000 copies in 1920–1921, for which Fitzgerald received $11,800. His income was usually exaggerated in the press.

could tell me of the intimate side of Fitzgerald. Being charmed with *This Side of Paradise*, and with the remarkable promise it evinced I wanted to know something of the person who wrote it other than that which was appearing in the literary supplements and magazines. From numerous opinions of him given by people who knew him and his family I conjectured that in some way he had ruffled the composure of his fellow townsmen. It might have been, I thought, that he refused to pronounce the name of the city of his birth in the provincial way. But he had done something, I was sure.

One of his friends of an earlier day, replying to a question I had asked, told me: "Yes, I know Scott very well. He is an awful snob." Another reported that at the present time he was sequestered in a New York apartment with $10,000 sunk in liquor and that he was bent on drinking it before he did anything else.

Still another related the story of how in New York, Fitzgerald became bored with his guests and called the fire department. When the firemen arrived and asked where the fire was Scott pounded his stomach and dramatically announced: "The fire is right here. Inside me."

One or two admitted that "Scottie was a great boy" but further than that they would not pledge themselves. That all of these cheerfully thrown handsful of mud could be true I doubted. Further I was a little put out with my kind informants because, I reflected, I could have imagined more lurid stories than those myself.

Then one day someone told me that Fitzgerald was coming to St. Paul to spend the winter. He was to take a house at White Bear until the weather got cold and then he was to move into the city. Eager to meet him I awaited the opportunity with a great deal of interest.

But when the time came it was on one of those torrid days of late summertime when the collar around one's neck becomes a wriggling snake with a hot stocky belly. With persistency born of madness the sun had beaten down on the low roof of the newspaper office for seven or eight hours. Shapes of blue smoke seemed to hover just below the ceiling and these, reinforced by voluminous puffs of dark smoke made by the machinery in the composing room, so completely clogged the wind-pipe that breathing was made a business to be engaged in with great seriousness. The typewriter before which I sat balked like an army mule whenever I essayed to strike a letter-key; the hot stickiness of the room had permeated its joints and whenever it allowed itself to be conquered, made an impression on the copy paper that was no more than a blur.

Thoroughly disgusted, I was all for calling it a day when a close acquaintance walked into the office and said: "Scott Fitzgerald is out at White Bear. Let's go out and see him." Had the day been less stifling I would have been more impressed. As it was I managed only to answer that as no place in the world could be hotter than the office where I then was I would be glad to drive out with him to meet Mr. Fitzgerald.

We were soon on our way and as we rode past the small pumpkin-planted farms the various rumors that I had heard concerning Fitzgerald came to my mind. I judged that if they were true he would appear rather dissipated. No one could drink a thousand bottles of liquor in one year without having a red nose and a blue-veined face! Not even Anton Dvořák.[2] Nor could anyone, because he was bored with his guests, telephone a hurry call to the fire department and not show that he was a peculiar person. These thoughts, and others of more marvelous fabric, engaged me as we plowed through the necessary ten miles of white smoky dust to reach White Bear.

"Now that we are here how are we going to find the house?" my friend wanted to know and I was about to tell him that we might ask at the Yacht club, when a Ford laundry delivery truck coughed past. We hailed the driver and explained our difficulty. "You wish to be directed to the home of Mr. Scott Fitzgerald the novelist," he answered in a high voice. "Well, if you'll just follow behind me I will take you there because I am delivering some laundry to them." We thanked him and drew our car in rear of his and in this way we reached a modestly proportioned house whose color, setting and architecture was admirably suited for a summer home.

Grasping a bottle of synthetic gin firmly around the neck I preceded my friend out of the car and up the path to the house. A voice answering the sound of the bell announced: "I'll be down in a minute." It was a strong boyish voice that could not have ascended from a liquor-parched throat. Another literary legend punctured.

Out on the enclosed porch, with the bottle of gin resting on a table beside us, we waited for the appearance of Mr. Fitzgerald. In a few minutes he came and, on seeing us, exclaimed to me: "Why, I thought you'd be wearing a frock coat and a long white beard."

I scanned him closely. His eyes were blue and clear; his jaw was squared at the end which perceptibly protruded; his nose was straight and his mouth, though sensitive looking, was regular in outline. His hair which was corn

---

[2] Composer Dvořák was a notable drinker.

colored, was wavy. His were the features that the average American mind
never fails to associate with beauty. But there was a quality in the eye with
which the average mind is unfamiliar. It amounted to—

"I thought you would be a baby with rouged lips,[3] so I too am disappointed," I told him.

We resumed our seats while he visited the kitchen, returning in a few
minutes with lemons, oranges, and cracked ice. I was surprised that he only
brought two glasses. "I suppose that's synthetic gin you've got there. Will
you have lemon or orange." We named our choice, and while squeezing the
juice of an orange into a glass turned and said: "You like Mencken, don't
you?"

"That would be like saying that I like the law of gravity," I replied, "but I
suppose I would say yes.

"Speaking of Mencken," I resumed, "I thought I saw a Baltimore forefin-
ger in *This Side of Paradise*. There is hardly a good book these days without
it."

"Well!" he replied, "I don't think *Main Street* would have been written if
Mencken hadn't been born. There are pages in that book that read just like
the Repitition Generale,[4] but that isn't true with *This Side of Paradise*. It was
not until after I had got the proofs of my book from the publishers that I
learned of Mencken. I happened across the *Smart Set* one day and I thought
'Here's a man whose name I ought to know. I guess I'll stick it in the proof
sheets.'[5] But I've met Mencken since then and I'm glad I put his name in.
Have you ever met him?"

I sorrowfully replied that I had not, but that I meant to some day.

"Gee, he's great. He's the one man in America for whom I have a complete
respect."

"But what is he like?" I wanted to know.

"Well, he's like a good natured beer-drinking German whom you would
imagine liking to sit around in his stocking feet."

"I can conceive of him being good-natured and liking to drink beer, if it is
good beer, but somehow the shoeless feet won't fit in. I suppose it's because
he plays the piano or else I have the orthodox complex. But he certainly has
made many things possible for the younger generation."

---

[3] Description attributed to Neysa McMein, artist and magazine illustrator.

[4] A regular section in *The Smart Set*, edited by Mencken and George Jean Nathan.

[5] An unlikely claim; Fitzgerald had submitted his writings to *The Smart Set* before *This
Side of Paradise* was in proof.

"Yes, you bet he has. He even helped boost Floyd Dell's *Moon-Calf* into success.[6] There's a book which certainly touches the depths of banality. He hasn't even a pretense of style and his manner of dumping his youthful history into the reader's lap with such a profound air of importance is simply disgusting. No, for once Mencken made a mistake."

At the time I was a Dell enthusiast so I took Fitzgerald's criticism with a gulp. I had nothing on the subject to offer in return and the conversation was as self-conscious as a fish out of water; my mind grasped at the first thought that entered my head.

"Sandburg," I said. "What do you think of Sandburg?"

And again my choice was horrific.

"Sandburg is probably an intelligent fellow. But to say that he is a poet is rot. The great city of Chicago felt a literary awakening and they looked around for a verse writer to call great. Sandburg was the only one in sight and immediately the legend of the great poet of the proletariat was built up to fit the shoulders of Sandburg."

But this time my position was not untenable.

"But, I don't agree with you there," I said. "Sandburg is a great poet. There are only two or three great poets in America and surely Sandburg is one of them."

"But he doesn't write any great lines. Tell me one of his verses that stick in your mind like Keats' 'Ode on a Grecian Urn.'"

"Well, there's 'Five Towns on the B. and O.'"

"All right, say it."

And I tried and failed. It may have been the fourth synthetic gin and orange juice concoction but my tongue would go no further than: "Hungry smoky shanties hanging to the slope."

"See there, you can't do it. And what kind of a poet is a man who can't make lines to stick in your head. Why even Vachel Lindsay—."[7]

And he started off a verse from the "Chinese Nightingale."

"From that point of view probably you're right, but Sandburg works otherwise. He makes his poems so that in their entirety they are ravishing. They are a complete thing in themselves. You see in them lyricism. The whole drama of the human race unfolds when he recites one of his verses."

"Why he's not half as lyrical as the feet of Charlie Chaplin."

---

[6] Fitzgerald strongly disliked this 1920 novel.

[7] Popular American poet who gave dramatic readings.

"Well, if you're going to drag in Charlie Chaplin's pathetic feet I can't discuss Sandburg with you any more. I should like to see Chaplin because I admire his work much, but I detest the whole caboodle of the movies outside of him. Consequently, I am seldom aware when a picture of his is showing in town."

"But you might as well protest against a Cunarder or the income tax as to protest against the movies," said Fitzgerald. "The movies are here to stay."

"Yes, I suppose they are, but then so is *Uncle Tom's Cabin*. By the way, what do you think of Ben Hecht[8] as a writer?"

"Oh, I like the things of his that I've seen very much. I'm looking forward to his novel that's coming out this fall. *Erik Dorn*, I think is the name of it."

"*Erik Dorn*, yes. So am I looking out for it. I remember seeing one of Hecht's plays shown at a ragamuffin theater in Chicago. It was about a hungry bum who was spending the night on the sidewalk. Toward morning as he was passing a plate glass window in a store he saw his reflection and exclaimed: 'Well, I'm a cock-eyed son-of-a-gun, if it ain't Jesus.' I thought it was good."

"That's funny. I've no doubt that Hecht will do wonders in fiction, but the author whose book I want to see most is John Dos Passos."

"Oh yes, I heard about his book. It's called *Three Soldiers*, isn't it?"

"That's it, and I've a hunch that it will be one of the best, if not the best book of the year," Fitzgerald said enthusiastically.[9]

Three months later that proved to be a very wise prediction.

"I've got Charles Norris's new novel in the house. John Farrar, of the *Bookman* sent it to me for review. Have you seen it?"

I replied that I had read the book and that I thought it very good.

"Well, what did you like about it? It didn't seem to me to touch his first book."

"Well, the question of marriage is a rather important one and for one to write a novel, or what Norris would call an interpretative novel of marriage, in which the author fails to take sides either for or against marriage and divorce, is quite an achievement. And then Norris makes his characters into real human beings. That's more than many fictionists do."

"Maybe you're right. But I can't see much in it. The grouping isn't clever

---

[8] Chicago newspaperman and novelist.

[9] Fitzgerald warmly reviewed *Three Soldiers* in the 25 September 1921 *St. Paul Daily News*.

and he has loaded his book with too many characters. It's too much like a brief."

"Norris can take care of himself. Tell me about your new novel. I've read the first installment of it in the *Metropolitan*."

"It's something after the manner of *Linda Condon*. Hergesheimer tried to show the effect on a woman after her once legitimate beauty had passed. That is what I am trying to do with Gloria."

"But that isn't all, is it?"

"No, that isn't all, but you wait and read it." He disappeared into the house and returned with the manuscript of *The Beautiful and Damned*. "Here it is."

It was written on ordinary-sized paper and not typed. The pencil scrawl was in large letters and altogether it must have been two feet thick. "This thing must be almost 200,000 words," I thought. After I had finished reading the first chapter, (he writes legibly,) I remarked that the manuscript was not very much like the printed story in the *Metropolitan*.

"Look here," I said, "this is much better than the *Metropolitan* version. There were some excellent descriptive passages entirely left out in the part that I read."

"Well," he looked in rather a funny way, "they bought the rights to do anything they liked with it when they paid for it."

"Of course it will appear as it was originally written when it comes out in book form, won't it?"

"Surely it will. I only hope—" and then he was silent.

"But good lord, if I were you I'd go around telling people that the original story was different from the *Metropolitan* story. Why, that *Metropolitan* story," I confessed, "was nothing but cheap sensationalism without any coherence at all."

As he offered no remark on the subject I turned the conversation. "What started you writing?"

"I've written ever since I can remember. I wrote short stories in school here, I wrote plays and poetry in prep school and I wrote plays and short stories for the Triangle and the *Lit* at Princeton. But Hugh Walpole was the man who started me writing novels. One day I picked up one of his books while riding on a train from New York to Washington. After I had read about 100 pages I thought that 'if this fellow can get away with it as an author I can too.' His books seemed to me to be as bad as possible. The principal thing he did was to make unessentials seem important, but he was one of the near-bestsellers. After that I dug in and wrote my first book."

"Well, you are probably right about Walpole and you may be right about Floyd Dell, but I think you're wrong about Charlie Norris and I know you're wrong about Sandburg. The trouble is you don't get Sandburg. It's the same way with Sherwood Anderson. Now that Anderson has been boosted so long by really intelligent persons the pretenders are beginning to praise him and ascribe motives to his work of which I know he never dreamed. There's something to Sandburg, a lot. I wish I could tell you about it, but it's not clear enough in my mind."

"I sure wish I could see it. If the man even wrote as well as Vachel Lindsay—you can remember Lindsay's stuff. 'Booth led boldly with a big bass drum.'"[10]

"But that's only cheap alliteration and it comes from a howling Methodist Y.M.C.A. proselyte to right-living. You can't seriously consider him."

But just then another automobile horn sounded from the gravel path and we prepared to leave. St. Paul already was paying homage to success! The sight of the large automobile stopping in front of the Fitzgerald home was an inspirational sight, I reflected. People will go ten miles to warm themselves in the warm rays thrown off by his glory. Oh, well, it were better that the singer of beauty be honored even at the cost of annihilation of the decalogue rather than that it be left to its own devices.

Our trip to town was a pleasant one. For some unaccountable reason a slight breeze ruffled the leaves of the trees and so I was deposited at my apartment in a not ill humor.

Later that evening I seated myself before a typewriter and filled four sheets of copy paper with an account of my visit with Fitzgerald. I began with my first impression of him, of how he had appeared at the head of the stairs clad in a suit of Alice-blue pajamas and I closed the interview warning him to watch the careers of Robert W. Chambers, Rupert Hughes, and Richard Harding Davis.[11] I also accused him of writing solely for money and of making a bid for the bestseller class. This interview, with a large photograph of Fitzgerald and his wife, was published in the St. Paul Daily News the following Sunday.

The following Monday the fellow who had driven me to White Bear met Fitzgerald at lunch, and he later reported to me that Fitzgerald thought my published interview with him "rather stupid." Probably it was; there seems

---

[10] From "General William Booth Enters into Heaven" (1913).

[11] Best-selling American novelists in the early years of the twentieth century.

to be no necessity for my having said that when he greeted me he was dressed in a suit of Alice-blue pajamas. It depressed me for a time because I was honestly anxious to form a friendship with this young man and it now seemed that such a thing was out of the question. But my apprehension was incorrect as I discovered in the course of a chance meeting with Fitzgerald a few days later. He was very cordial and failed to make mention of the interview in any way.

In all phases of life and probably in after-life every state of existence, no matter how onerous, seems to possess some recompense. In Hell one is entirely separated from the godly; in heaven there are, so we are told, no functioning congressmen nor any police officers; a dweller in an apartment is not bothered with shoveling coal; in the South Sea Islands, if we are to believe Paul Gauguin and Frederick O'Brien,[12] there are no rentals, taxes of storekeepers to be taken into account. But in Minnesota, even the climate is adamantine in its stern Christian resolve to keep its inhabitants from falling into the ways of pleasure. So we were plunged from a hot disagreeable summer into a cold frozen winter that left one with the alternative of skating and tobogganing parties or feeding the hungry red mouth of the residential furnace all evening.

Last year was no exception and the Fitzgerald family gave up the summer place rather early and removed to one of the new apartment hotels here. After that we saw each other daily. Scott was at that time beginning a comedy for the stage and he felt that his work would be less interrupted if he rented an office in a downtown business building. His new novel *The Beautiful and Damned* had appeared in its last instalment in a popular magazine and Fitzgerald had suggested that I should not read it until I could read the entire book.

He had been hard at work rewriting parts of the original story and changing it to advantage so that it would be ready for publication in book form by March 3. He had also written three or four short stories. Two of them he sold to popular magazines and the price he got for one, he told me, was $1,500. And there he worked nearly every day on his play. And yet people with the utmost seriousness report stories of Fitzgerald's abandoned carousals that to hear them tell it happened every day. Any extraordinary person in the mind of the ordinary man must have a thirst like a camel and a belly the size of an elephant. Even such a lesser light as Woodrow Wilson has been killed by too

---

[12] American travel writer, author of *White Shadows in the South Seas* (1919).

much liquor and ladies—by the populace. So must the vulgar ever prate. Of course, the obvious reason for all this is that the public ever must associate the author with the principal character in the books he writes. So, if the principal character takes an occasional drink or winks an eye at a pretty woman the author of the book necessarily must be a low fellow with a morality of a libertine and the taste of a bar-fly. One never associates lewd stories and midnight parties with Dr. Frank Crane and Orison Swett Marden[13] though they are as likely to indulge in them as George Moore[14] and Marcel Proust.

Enthusiasm runs high in the nature of Fitzgerald. He is even enthusiastic in his dislikes and certainly he is whole hearted over the things that he enjoys. To be with him for an hour is to have the blood in one's veins thawed and made fluent. His bright humor is as infectious as smallpox and as devastating to gloom. He has humor all right, someone may remark, but it is never shown when he is made the butt of it. Of course, it isn't. He is not enough of a dissimulator for that. What person honestly does enjoy being made the butt of a joke? I have searched far but the man still remains a bird of paradise. Some persons, when a joke is made at their expense, will smile, but the mouth will droop in one corner, like a courageous prize-fighter who has been struck a sharp blow on the nose. No, the entire psychology of the joke is against one's smiling at one's own expense. Where is the "sudden glory" of which Max Eastman[15] speaks? How can one appreciate the "cracker" when it knocks out three of his front teeth?

At this time a man passed through St. Paul who had years ago, written three or four good books, but since had almost completely stopped writing to devote his time to drink.

One day after we left him and were walking up the street Scott remarked:

"There goes one of the last survivors of the 'booze and inspiration' school. Bret Harte was one of the earliest ones and it was all right in his day, but the old school of writers who learned to drink and to write while reporting for a newspaper is dying out. Do you remember the story of how Harte, visiting Mark Twain in California, said one night that he had to write a story and get it to the publisher the next afternoon?"

I replied that I might have heard it, but if I had I must have forgotten.

"Well, Bret Harte came to Mark Twain's home one afternoon for a visit

---

[13] Crane and Marden were American inspirational writers.

[14] Moore was a major literary figure in the "Irish Renaissance" at the turn of the century.

[15] Liberal magazine editor and writer.

and after he had been there a few hours he said that he had to write a story that night because he had promised the publishers of a magazine that he would have it for them in the morning. So Twain suggested that Harte could use his study, but Harte said, 'Oh no, I've got plenty of time. Let's talk a while.'

"They killed most of the afternoon talking and after dinner Twain again suggested that Harte go up to his study and start to work. But again Harte was not ready. 'There's no rush. Let's talk a while longer.'

"After a while it got to be 1 o'clock and Twain becoming sleepy, told Harte that he was going to bed and asked him whether he wanted anything before he started to work.

"'Well,' said Harte. 'If you'll have a fire made in the study and a quart of whisky sent up I'll be all right.'

"So Twain went to bed and Harte to the study. About 5 o'clock in the morning a servant was called and another fire was made in the room and another bottle of whisky was brought in. At 9 o'clock Harte came downstairs to breakfast with the story of 6,000 words, completed.

"But that gang is not to be met anymore. I can't think of how he could have done it. For me, narcotics are deadening to work. I can understand anyone drinking coffee to get a stimulating effect, but whisky—oh, no."

"*This Side of Paradise* doesn't read as if it were written on coffee," I remarked.

"And it wasn't. You'll laugh, but it was written on Coca-Cola. Coca-Cola bubbles up and fizzes inside enough to keep me awake."

Imagine Amory Blaine being born of a Coca-Cola mother! But it is exuberant and sparkling enough to have been at that.

Fitzgerald's apartment was perhaps twenty minutes walk from his office and, when there was not too much snow on the ground, he would walk rather than take the streetcar. From this, many people got the idea that he positively refused to ride on the streetcar and many of them began to uphold him in what they considered another of his eccentricities.

His writing is never thought out. He creates his characters and they are likely to lead him into almost any situation. His phrasing is done in the same way. It is rare that he searches for a word. Most of the time words come to his mind and they spill themselves in a riotous frenzy of song and color all over the page. Some days he writes as many as 7,000 or 8,000 words; and then, with a small *Roget's Thesaurus*, he carefully goes over his work, substituting synonyms for any unusual words that appear more than once in seven or eight consecutive pages. Bernard Shaw has said that no one should write until he can supply at least five synonyms for any word that comes into his mind. Mr. Shaw says that he is able to do that, but it is not an entirely wild speculation to venture that if anyone entered the Shaw study sometimes he might see a well thumbed thesaurus lying around.

Fitzgerald is extraordinarily curious. To that quality in him is due the responsibility for a number of the legends that have been built up around him. To illustrate:

We had gone into a cigar store to roll dice for a package of cigarettes. Fitzgerald rolled the dice first and the highest combination that turned was three of sixes. I must have been standing on a four leafed clover because when I threw the dice I was apportioned four treys. But Fitzgerald did not notice. A blind man, feeling his way along with walking stick, had come in the door and Fitzgerald was watching him as if he were a unique fact. "You lose," I called. "I've got four treys," but he did not hear. So I paid the cigar man for both packages and we went out into the street. I noticed that Fitzgerald was acting queerly as we stepped on the sidewalk. He seemed quite unsteady on his feet and, as I looked up, I saw that he had closed his eyes. Silently, I watched him walk down the crowded street, feeling his way along by tapping against the sides of the buildings with his walking stick. A young woman, passing in company with a man, exclaimed, "Oh look at that poor boy. How sad it must be to be blind." But Fitzgerald walked on, his eyes shut. He had almost experienced the sensations of a blind man for an entire block on a crowded street when unluckily, two middle aged women passed us by and passing, one said to the other: "Oh look at that." And then Fitzgerald opened his eyes.

I told you he was curious. When he discovered that the woman's ejaculation had been caused by the sight of a bargain window in a department store he was furious.

"It's perhaps just as well that no one recognized you else you would be reported to have blind staggers," I said to him.

"Didn't I walk very well—as well as the blind man?" His voice was truculent.

"No you didn't. It is remarkable that you didn't knock your brains out. There were a number of times when I started to take hold of your arm to keep some passerby from knocking you down."

At that he seemed rather downcast, but he almost immediately cheered up, thinking, no doubt, that he could sell his experiences to some popular magazine.

Fitzgerald is hardly what Miss Fanby Hurst[16] calls an "Art for God Saker." He writes his books because he has something to write about and it pleases him that he has written them, but if they were not to sell at least 50,000 copies he would feel cheated and highly indignant. Two or three times he has written stories with no other purpose in mind than to sell them. To explain: he took the plot of an old story and made it fit the pattern of the kind of thing that is known today as the short story. It is a simple matter to rewrite a story that has been published some fifty years ago and it is as easy to sell it if the story is properly enough clothed in a modern dress. But much more often he writes solely to please himself and the result may be seen in such yarns as "Dalrymple Goes Wrong," which sets forth the thought that if a returned soldier can't get honest work to support himself he had better find dishonest work because poverty is the greatest crime in the world. Arnold Bennett, the great English novelist, by the way, uses the same idea as the motif of his latest novel. Or again, Fitzgerald, through his stories, will take you through a highly imaginative land of his own creation which he has made half with sheer fun and half with keen satire.

About three months ago Fitzgerald decided that he would write a play. He had written a number of them for his class at the University of Princeton, but they were more or less nothing but prettily blended handsful of confetti. This play, that he was now going to write, he planned, would have a long run at some Broadway theater and then tour the country for a year or so. He finished it in six weeks and, as it is a highly original comedy of the kind that America needs most of all, some discerning man such as Harris or Frohman is probably getting it ready for production.[17]

Fitzgerald, perhaps subconsciously, realizes that America has never learned how properly to smile. And so he is going to teach America to turn up the corners of its mouth, both of them at the same time.

Apparently the editors of the magazine in which *The Beautiful and Damned* was published slashed every line from the novel that was not sensational. Kissing matches, cocktail parties and similar bordel bait were handled in a manner suggestive of Town Topics; excellent descriptive passages were

---

[16] Fannie Hurst was an American sentimental novelist.

[17] The play, which failed during its Atlantic City tryout in November 1923, was not produced by leading Broadway producers William Harris and Charles Frohman but instead by Sam H. Harris.

clipped from the story by a hand seemingly barbarous enough to whitewash
the Mona Lisa. There seemed to be no idea, certainly no definite plan to the
book. It was like a necklace with a broken cord, the jewels scattered carelessly over the floor.

And that is unfortunate because many intelligent persons, lured into purchase of this magazine because they were attracted by Scott's first novel, *This
Side of Paradise*, will have read the instalment-by-instalment novel and be-
lieving the book to be identical with the serialization, will not read the book.

Ergo: it is no more than just that readers must be set aright with regard to
events that inspire, and the manner in which they are written within the pages
of *The Beautiful and Damned*, published by the Scribner's March 1.

Figures of speech swiftly flap their wings toward the open door of his
mind; all that Scott has to do is to choose discriminately among them. Words
rush pell-mell from his pencil end and spill themselves in a frenzy of brilliant
colors over the manuscript of the new novel, the short story or the play on
which he is practicing his rich and unusual talents. Physically and mentally
he is orderly; this is evidenced in his books, particularly in *The Beautiful and
Damned*, a book which is, to my mind, one of the best pieces of sustained
coherence that I have read. In it there is an idea, logically presented and
faithfully carried out, that implies utter disillusionment.

Anthony Patch and Gloria, the principal characters in the book, are firmly
and illuminatingly limned; old Adam Patch, Anthony's grandfather, a man of
many millions and a contributor to Comstockery, is as sharply drawn a character as my imagination can conceive. A pity we see so little of him. Dick is
the blush of perfection for asininity; he seems a composite of a number of
persons. I hazard a guess and say—Rupert Hughes, the author—whom else,
I know not. At any rate, he is the least distinct character in the book. At times
he is a flabby-handed Y.M.C.A. lobby-lounging right-thinker. At other times,
he has flashes of sophistication and humaneness (then he is F. S. F.), again he
is a conceited—well, I give it up. Maury Noble seems somewhat vague and
shadowy, remembered chiefly for the hand he waves, pawlike, in a gesture of
negation.

Only in Theodore Dreiser's *Sister Carrie* is the disintegration of a man
shown with more bludgeoning effect. The final scenes are poignant, relent-
less, and extraordinarily vivid; the last one ends on a plaintive wailing note.

After reading his first novel, *This Side of Paradise*, and then his collection
of short stories which followed, I suspected Scott of being weak in the quality
of imagination—I mean that *This Side of Paradise* seemed largely autobio-

graphical and the stories, as a whole, were rewritten tales—but the suspicion completely disappeared when I read such bits as the Chevalier O'Keefe fantasy, the training camp episode, both of which appear in his book, and his story, "The Diamond in the Sky,"[18] which comes out in *Smart Set*.

The chapter headings captivate one with the insouisance of them and their aptitude is to be marveled at. In them is the quality that one likes best in the book: youth sparkling with the joy of life, revelling in pagan beauty, demanding everything and giving in return everything it has despite itself.

I am no prognosticator, but I believe that *The Beautiful and Damned*, deservedly, will be this season's most successful book.

---

[18] Fitzgerald retitled his story "The Diamond as Big as the Ritz."

F. Scott Fitzgerald, Novelist, Shocked by "Younger Marrieds" and Prohibition[1]

Marguerite Mooers Marshall / 1922

Reprinted from the *New York Evening World,* 1 April 1922, p. 3.

"New York is going crazy! When I was here a year ago I thought we'd seen the end of night life. But now it's going on as it never was before Prohibition. I'm confident that you can find anything here that you find in Paris. Everybody is drinking harder—that's sure. Possessing liquor is a proof of respectability, of social position. You can't go anywhere without having your host bring out his bottle and offer you a drink. He displays his liquor as he used to display his new car or his wife's jewels. Prohibition, it seems to me, is having simply a ruinous effect on young men."

It is a young man himself who is speaking—no clergyman, no social reformer, but a "regular" young man. Most of you know his name—F. Scott Fitzgerald, who wrote *This Side of Paradise,* a book that managed to be both brilliant and popular, when he was just out of Princeton, two years ago; whose second novel, *The Beautiful and Damned*, is newly published. (A reader of both suggests that, in view of the first tale, the second could have been called, consistently, "Next Stop Is Hell!")

The frank Mr. Fitzgerald undoubtedly set the fashion of holding the mirror up to the flapper. Some of us, in two years, have grown a bit weary of studying her reflection. So we welcome the fact that, in his second novel, Mr. Fitzgerald turns his attention to other representatives of his generation—to the "younger marrieds," in the locution of the society columns. They outflap the flapper! With youth, health, beauty, love, friends, money, pleasure, his Anthony and Gloria, typifying the prosperous, newly married couple in New York, are hopelessly, irretrievably "damned," broken in body and spirit; one an accomplished, the other an incipient dipsomaniac, before the end of the story.

---

[1] In an undated letter to Marshall, Fitzgerald wrote, "I liked your interview immensely. Thank you for the publicity which it gave me—but mostly for the interest which inspired you to write it." Rendell Catalogue Number 267.

"But why?" I asked the young novelist, when I met him at the Plaza Hotel, where he and his wife are staying for a few days. Their home is in St. Paul, Minn. "In some ways your pair were a special case. But we all know scores of young men and women here in New York who marry under the happiest auspices, and who, in a few years, manage to throw away all their chances of lifelong happiness and security together. What is the matter with our young married couples?"

"First of all, I think it's the way everybody is drinking," replied the blue-eyed, frank-faced, fastidiously dressed author. His stories are world weary, but he himself is as clean and fresh and boyish as if he'd never had an idea or a disillusion. Then he gave the candid, impartial impression of New York life of the present quoted at the beginning of this interview.

"There's the philosophy of ever so many young people to-day," he went on, thoughtfully. "They don't believe in the old standards and authorities, and they're not intelligent enough, many of them, to put a code of morals and conduct in place of the sanctions that have been destroyed for them. They drift. Their attitude toward life might be summed up: 'This is ALL. Then what does it matter? We don't care! Let's GO!'"

A little nervous movement of Mr. Fitzgerald's cigarette finished the sentence.

The young wife in his book remarks, even before entering the state of matrimony, that she does not want to have responsibility and a lot of children to take care of. "Evidently," observes her creator, with a nuance of sarcasm, "she did not doubt that on her lips all things were good." So I asked him how far he considered the young married woman to blame for the "damnation" of her own life and that of her husband.

"She's very largely to blame," he responded promptly. "Our American women are leeches. They're an utterly useless fourth generation trading on the accomplishment of their pioneer great-grandmothers. They simply dominate the American man. You should see the dowagers trailing around this hotel with their dependent males! No Englishman would endure one-eighth of what an American takes from his wife.

"I've often asked myself the question, 'To what is a woman entitled from life?' The answer, obviously, is 'All she can get!' And when she marries she gets the whole thing. She makes a man love her, then proceeds to hog all his emotions, to get all the money out of him she can, to keep him at her beck and call. She makes a monkey of him, in many cases, and he has to stand it unless he wants a continuous verbal battle."

Mr. Fitzgerald took another whiff of his cigarette.

"What chance have they, these men and women of my generation who come from families with some money!" he exclaimed. "I'm not blaming them. What chance has the young man, unless he has to work for his living? If he were born in England there would at least be a tradition behind him and a background. Here he is born in a Middle Western town. His grandfather, perhaps, was a farm laborer. He—the third generation—is brought up to be absolutely helpless. He is sent to a fine private school, near New York, and before he's through he knows everything every boy ever knew and every chorus girl in town. His idea of happiness is to have one of them on the back seat of a limousine. Then his family resolves that he must go to Yale. He goes there to raise hell. When he's through—if he gets through—he's absolutely ruined.

"He ought to do something. But what can he do? Suppose he thinks that he might try to help govern his country." But what he would think next is so perfectly summed up in *The Beautiful and Damned* that I shall quote it word for word:

> He tried to imagine himself in Congress, rooting around in the litter of that incredible pigsty, with the narrow and porcine brows he saw pictured sometimes, those glorified proletarians babbling blandly to the Nation the ideas of high school seniors! Little men with copy-book ambitions who by mediocrity had thought to emerge from mediocrity into the lustreless and unromantic heaven of a government by the people—and the best, the dozen shrewd men at the top, egotistic and cynical, were content to lead this choir of white ties and wire collarbuttons in a discordant and amazing hymn, compounded of a vague confusion between wealth as a reward of virtue and wealth as a proof of vice, and continued cheers for God, the Constitution and the Rocky Mountains!

"Nevertheless," I said, "all our younger married set cannot be 'damned.' Surely you can suggest some way in which they may be 'saved'?"

"Work!" at once exclaimed Mr. Fitzgerald, his blue eyes earnest. "Work is the one salvation for all of us—even if we must work to forget there's nothing worth while to work for, even if the work we turn out—books, for example—doesn't satisfy us. The young man must work. His wife must work"—

"How?" I interrupted. "At bringing up an old-fashioned family?"

Scott Fitzgerald IS a boy, and married happily, and not too long.

"I think," he confided, ingenuously, "that just being in love, really in love—doing it well, you know—is work enough for a woman. If she keeps her house the way it should be kept and makes herself look pretty when her husband comes home in the evening and loves him and helps him with his work and encourages him—oh, I think that's the sort of work that will save her. It's not so easy, you know, being in love and making it go."

Evidently the younger generation, whatever the vagaries of its head, still believes in keeping its heart in the same old place!

Fitzgerald Condemns St. Paul Flappers: "Unattractive, Selfish, Graceless," Are Adjectives Applied to Middle West Girls

John O'Donnell / 1922

Reprinted from the *St. Paul Daily News,* 16 April 1922, sec. 1, pp. 1, 5.

Now let the wrath of St. Paul flappers descend upon F. Scott Fitzgerald!

In the matter of attractiveness, middle west girls (and St. Paul is in the middle west) rank at the bottom of the list, according to the young St. Paul authority on flappers.

Mr. Fitzgerald recently visited New York. There he was interviewed by various and sundry newspaper men. Perhaps he didn't know the interview would ever get back to St. Paul but it did—and here it is:

"And as for the girl of the middle west—"

F. Scott Fitzgerald inhaled deeply and paused before he released a cloud of cigaret smoke and a shower of burning adjectives.

"She is unattractive, selfish, snobbish, egotistical, utterly graceless, talks with an ugly accent and in her heart knows that she would feel more at home in a kitchen than in a ballroom."

The author who has been hailed as the interpreter of American youth halted for a moment. Fitzgerald, frankly good-looking, the hero of half a hundred proms, the realistic reporter of parlor fights and petting parties, plunged ahead into his analysis of the great American flapper.

"There is much of the uncouthness of the pioneer left in the middle western flapper," continued Fitzgerald. "She lacks the social grace of entertaining men. Her idea is to get everything and give nothing.

"There is in her a respect for the primitive feminine talents; she would really make a good cook but her family has made money in the last generation and there is no excuse for her to go into the kitchen. She doesn't know what she wants to do."

Fitzgerald should know. He was born in St. Paul. Furthermore, his judgment carries authority. For critics agree that the author of *This Side of Paradise* and *The Beautiful and Damned* understands women—flappers, at least.

"The southern girl is easily the most attractive type in America," continued Fitzgerald, with a wave of his cigarette. "Next the girl from the east. At the bottom of the list the middle-western flapper."

"Hasn't she any good points?" I asked rather hopefully.

"Yes. She has her health," he admitted.

"Now for the southern girl." Here Fitzgerald became enthusiastic. "First of all remember that I married a southern girl. A characteristic is that she retains and develops her ability to entertain men. The middle-western girls lack this utterly. With the sophisticated eastern girl, it is a give-and-take proposition.

"No matter how poor a southern girl may be, and many of them are very poor, she keeps up her social activities. In New York, when a girl's family loses its money, she drops out of the running. This is not true of the south.

"Can you imagine a New York girl having a good time at a prom when she knows that she is not so well or so expensively dressed as the other girls?

"Now in the south, the girls, because of their tradition of before-the-war culture—most of which is false—and their sense of old-world courtesy, know how to enjoy themselves despite financial embarrassment.

"A southern girl will slip into a simple muslin or organdie frock, go to a dance, entertain men on a rickety old porch, have a thoroughly good time and make no attempt to conceal her poverty. In fact, she will even boast of it.

"I remember one southern girl who delighted a crowd of young people by telling them of the efforts she made to prevent a maid from unpacking her trunk when she went to visit wealthy friends. She knew that the maid would be shocked to discover that she had placed cardboard in the bottoms of her worn-out shoes."

The Gossip Shop

The Bookman / 1922

Reprinted from *The Bookman,* 55 (May 1922), pp. 333–34.

A pale young man with pale blue eyes, and pale blond hair parted in the middle; a collegiate youth in New York trying to sell a play about a flapper—a "preposterous, rather common flapper" to use his own words. Trying also to find a beautiful young actress to play the lead in a Peter Pan-ish phantasy (perhaps that's why they picked the fashion editor to interview him). Three guesses as to the new dramatist! If you can't possibly guess we'll tell you that he's F. Scott Fitzgerald. He told us confidentially that he expected he'd be forced to pick a flapper off Fifth Avenue and train her to the part. We believe he'd do just that. So you may be discovered yet, Flavia. We hate to shatter any illusions, but Scottie did say—we heard him—that he does *not* like flappers, that he did not marry one—his wife's a "good egg"—and that he did not invent the term as it is used in America. The criminal in this case, says he, is Mr. H. L. Mencken.

He further confessed that he didn't know many authors; did we?—(was that our cue to pipe up, "We've just met one"?)—and that he wanted to. He had visited Joseph Hergesheimer: "He's an egoist but a nice egoist." Then in wandered Your Editor to talk of *Cytherea* and *Crome Yellow*.[1] Mr. Fitzgerald thinks Aldous Huxley great because he "kids everybody and kids himself, and kids himself for kidding himself and for kidding everybody,"—just there we lost track of his line, not unlike a sentence in *The Harbor*[2] about "making freighters to carry iron ore to make more freighters to carry iron ore, etc." Scott Fitzgerald makes gorgeous fun of himself; he has a trick of looking up swiftly and mischievously at you, anticipating a laugh. And we do like best in others our own characteristics. We laugh at ourselves all the time. It's the safe thing to do. Probably Mr. Fitzgerald does not do it for safety—he has no need to. Perhaps he does it because he's Irish.

---

[1] *Cytherea* (1922), novel by Hergesheimer; *Crome Yellow* (1921), novel by Huxley, which Fitzgerald reviewed.

[2] 1915 novel by Ernest Poole.

Fitzgerald, Flapperdom's Fiction Ace, Qualifies as Most Brilliant Author, But Needs Press Agent, Says Scribe

"Bart" Fulton / 1922

A Montgomery, Alabama, newspaper, ca. Fall 1922. Reprinted from Fitzgerald's scrapbook.

Howsoever magic may be his gift of thrilling American flapperdom, F. Scott Fitzgerald isn't the most easily interviewed person of consequence we have met.

Mr. Fitzgerald, his wife (Zelda Sayre), and babe of six months arrived in Montgomery the latter part of the week. New York with its chill winds and "passing shows" grows "boresome at this season of the year."

We were dispatched posthaste out to interview him. Scott, aside from being a celebrated fictionist, is a favorite in Montgomery as a consequence of his having turned to the capital city for a wife.

Montgomery would want to know firsthand what its adopted author had on his heart.

"I am going to be interviewed by the press," the blonde Minnesotan beamed to his wife, who smiled acquiescence.

Wouldn't the press be seated—have a smoke?

And the delightful young writer whose philosophy admits not of thrills, the dean of the school of sophistication, truly showed signs of enthusiasm.

Actually you would have believed the experience a novel one with him! But then we remembered a syndicated interview of his that appeared some six months ago in dailies the country over, in which he pictured the Southern girl the most charming of them all, the Eastern miss secondly so, the Middle Western lass, the girl of his native section, a fit housewife. (Scott says he'll stand by all he said relative to the charm of the girl from Dixie, but admits that they have not quite forgiven him in St. Paul, his home, for the things he's supposed to have said, but didn't, of the girl from the corn belt).

"I'll not talk of flappers. I can sell that sort of chatter," he observed.

"Prohibition is a dead issue. The war's over. Folks are tired of hearing of

33

the doings of Broadway, Europe and other points listed. Montgomery is no longer Southern, but progressive.

"So what shall be the chatter, beautiful?" (That's a pet name for "the brains of the family").

Mrs. Fitzgerald would "just wait until the press took a notion to interview her." She was disappointed! Why didn't the newspaper men recognize genius?

And we saw the author of *This Side of Paradise*, *Tales of the Jazz Age*, and other bits of literature and "near literature" wasn't coming through.

F. Scott Fitzgerald must needs depend upon his short stories for his press-agenting. He was too modest to ballyhoo himself into added fame through the columns of the newspaper.

"How did you ever happen to marry your wife?" we asked. Maybe the inside story of this had not reached all Montgomery readers.

"Ah! That's interesting," he smiled. Would "Beautiful" object if he told? She wouldn't.

"I met her at the Country Club at a dance—I was a lieutenant, you know, in the Ohio division—we quarreled. I sorta enjoyed quarreling with her. She was so clever about it.

"I went back to camp—I took inventory—I found there was something missing.

"I discovered the next morning at breakfast it was my heart. I would quarrel with 'Beautiful' again.

"A few nights later we met and had another pitched battle—words the weapons used.

"Then I went back home—we quarreled the night I left. And for the next few months carried on through the mails.

"It was not long before the editors decided they would use my stuff—this, after I had received 150 rejection slips—and then—

"Well, everyone knows the rest.

"I returned to 'Beautiful' and we were married and we've lived—happily—ever afterwards.

"That is, we expect to."

F. Scott Fitzgerald—Juvenile Juvenal of the Jeunesse Jazz

Roy L. McCardell / 1922

Reprinted from the *Morning Telegraph,* 12 November 1922, magazine section, p. 3.

Like Punch, young folks ain't what they used to be, and they never were.

If the hieroglyphics on the Central Park obelisk were truly deciphered, they would undoubtedly be found to state that the youth of Memphis, Karnak, Luxor, Thebes, and other towns up the Nile, were disobedient to their parents, disrespectful, disorderly, no longer amenable to law, order or discipline, and, in short, out of all bounds—both girls and boys—and going plumb to the devil and taking the whole country with them!

It was ever thus, the youngsters of an elder day were all right, and the youngsters of the present day were always wrong. When as we used to point with pride, now we can only view with alarm!

Francis Scott Key Fitzgerald—his forefathers were of old Maryland stock, Lord Baltimore brand, and he was named after the author of "The Star Spangled Banner"—is one of the youngest of the younger intelligentia, and he has gained his great renown writing books about the rising generation—rising to dance and sitting down to drink and rising to dance and sitting down to drink again.

Stories of sex and sex, and he just twenty-six!

F. Scott Fitzgerald, as he calls himself for short, was born in St. Paul, Minn., and resides there. But now that he is a successful author and the royalties are rolling in, he comes on to New York and puts up at the Plaza and looks on at metropolitan life among the wealthy rich, young and old, ever and anon. But he only writes about the young dancers and drinkers among the wealthy rich, as a general thing.

He was educated in the Newman School, Hackensack, N.J., and matriculated at Princeton University, but left college to join the war in 1917 and did not graduate.

He served as a shave tail—Second Looie Forty-fifth Infantry, and was afterward a First Looie in the Sixty-seventh Infantry and aide-de-camp to

35

Brigadier General J. A. Ryan—not O'Ryan—got a sore arm from saluting superior officers, but never got overseas.

After the war was over he got a job as copy writer in the advertising agency of Barron G. Collier, who is now a special deputy police commissioner. The Collier Agency specializes in street car advertising, and young Fitzgerald had to keep his stuff snappy.[1] He has a good, terse style of idiomatic English, and that's where he got it—the flavor lasts.

He only served three months writing snappy sentences for those who rode to read—those hard-boiled pessimists who never get a seat in street cars or the subway—for he sold two stories to the *Smart Set*, and decided to give up his regular job and go back to St. Paul and be a regular author.

A year later he published his first novel, *This Side of Paradise*. It registered a hit the first month it was off the press, and in the next month, on April 3, 1920, to be exact, our young author married Zelda Sayre, the beautiful, brilliant daughter of Judge and Mrs. A. D. Sayre, of Montgomery, Ala. The young folk had been engaged for a year and a half and were only waiting until the bridegroom-elect became a successful author to hop off.

Not only is F. Scott Fitzgerald a successful author and a successful husband at twenty-six, but he is the successful father of one dear little daughter just ten months old.

Of himself, he says:

"My first story, written at the age of twelve, was called 'Elavo.' It was a novel in verse about knights and Norman strongholds, drawbridges, seneshals, donjon keeps and such, and I give you three guesses as to what I had just been reading."

Three guesses? It is a cinch, Scott!

The short, snappy paragraph above is deep stuff for lowbrows, but those of the cognoscenti will wise it as a wow. A neat nifty; eh, what?

"I lived in St. Paul," young Fitzgerald goes on to say, "and aside from an unnatural egotism I was a normal, Middle Western boy who played marbles, football, baseball and flew a kite at the proper seasons, and gave a circus after the circus left and an exposition of amateur wizardry and handcuff king stuff after Kellar and Houdini had come and gone. I produced my own crook play at fifteen, after H. B. Warner had starred the twin towns in 'Alias Jimmy Valentine.'

---

[1] Fitzgerald claimed credit for the laundry slogan "We keep you clean in Muscatine." See Fitzgerald's 25 September 1936 *New York Evening Post* interview with Michel Mok, p. 124.

"After this I wrote several other horrible little plays that were given for charity and injudiciously commended by friends, fellow-participators, my misguided family and the local press. There were three of these dreadful productions from which nothing further developed except a sad case of swelled head for the author, but which in time subsided somewhat.[2]

"I then went to college and continued to think well of myself for quite a while. During my sophomore year at Princeton, Edmund Wilson, since an assistant editor to Frank Crowninshield on *Vanity Fair*, was pleased to say of me at the time: 'Scott Fitzgerald could make one play by Shaw, one novel by Meredith and one poem by Browning go further than most people could do with the reading of years!'

"Then I reformed and began to read enormously, but I am still shy on the classics. I have never read the *Iliad*, the *Odyssey*, the *Divine Comedy*, the *Cid* or *Faust*."

But he need not worry; nobody else has ever read them.

"The first version of *This Side of Paradise* I wrote in the officers' training camp when I was twenty-one. It was turned down by three publishers. I put it aside for a year and then rewrote and sold it. Then I got married and wrote my second novel, *Flappers and Philosophers*[3]; this was in 1920. In 1921 I published *The Beautiful and the Damned*,[4] and vast numbers of its readers cannot be convinced but what it, as well as my other novels of jazzing young America, is biographical."

The critics, one and all, from Mencken to Broun and from Burton Rascoe to Hildegarde Hawthorne, have acclaimed F. Scott Fitzgerald as a genius and not only arrived, but from whom we may expect even greater, better work.

"You may not like what he writes about," the critics say, "you may deplore the fact that most of his characters are rotters or weaklings, base or mean. That has nothing to do with the fact that he is a writer who it is a joy to read, and if he chooses to write for the moment of the life and the persons with which and whom he is most intimate, if he prefers to paint with startling vividness and virility the jazz aspect of the American scene, why not? Who can do it better—or as well?"

On the other hand, those who view with alarm both our riotous, unheeding

---

[2] The "crook play" was *The Girl from Lazy J,* produced in St. Paul in 1911. Fitzgerald's other three apprentice plays included *The Captured Shadow* (1912), *Coward* (1913), and *Assorted Spirits* (1914).

[3] *Flappers and Philosophers* is a collection of short stories, not a novel.

[4] *The Beautiful and Damned* was published in 1922.

young men and young women, their actions and reactions, are inclined to blame the F. Scott Fitzgerald school of fiction as much as the strident social saturnalias of Scotch and sex-consciousness that he chronicles.

We of the intelligentia—you said it—are more than certain that our dear, old friend Professor J. Duncan Spaeth—well, who is he?—was taking a nasty crack at our boy author when he said in the *Trend*—yes, it's a Philadelphia magazine, but who reads it?:

> The characteristic note of temporary American fiction is that it combines the disillusionment of age with the waywardness of youth. It is smart without being wise, bold without being adventurous, petulant without being revolutionary, incapable alike of the frank and honest cynicism of disenchanted age and of the frank and honest enthusiasm of enchanted youth. It is sophisticated and half-baked at the same time; it is wrinkled before it has ripened!

Well, suppose Professor Spaeth is right, what difference does it make, what have these things to do with life and literature? Let us remember that the newest egg is bald, the youngest prune is wrinkled!

And there are other discordant notes—vituperative letters, to instance. The greetings are never wholly paeans of praise. Of course, a popular young author gets any amount of letters of adulation, but ever and anon, to spoil the day, he will get a nasty slam like this:

> F. Scott Fitzgerald:
> Sir—I have read your story, "Benjamin Button," in *Collier's*, and I want to say that as a writer you are a good lunatic. I have seen many big pieces of cheese in my time, but you are the biggest, and I don't know why I waste this paper and my time on you, but I will.
> Sincerely, Your Friend and Constant Reader.

F. Scott Fitzgerald's last volume, *Tales of the Jazz Age*, is a collection of his recent short stories and novelettes, including "May Day," "A Sordid Study,"[5] and "The Lees of Happiness." This last is tragic, after the Greek fashion, because the fates were unkind and protagonists of the story helpless in their grasp. But the volume contains burlesque and spoofery as well, and tales of extravagance and burlesque added also in the plethora of the author's

---

[5] Fitzgerald did not publish a story of this title.

versatility. These tales in a lighter vein include "The Camel's Back," "Jemima," and "The Diamond as Big as the Ritz."

F. Scott Fitzgerald prefers piquant hors d'oeuvres to a hearty meal. He also is fond of Charlie Chaplin, Booth Tarkington, real Scotch, old-fashioned hansom cab riding in Central Park and the "Ziegfeld Follies." He admires Mencken and Nathan, Park & Tilford, Lord & Taylor, Lea & Perrins, the Smith Brothers, and Mrs. Gibson, the pig lady, and her Jenny mule.[6]

He prefers Fifth Avenue to Piccadilly and the Champs Elysees.

Further than this he presents and urges no claim to be seriously considered except as a handsome young man, a nice young fellow, a successful young author, and a good young husband and father, except that he realized at the first showing that William Fox was the mysterious Mr. X., author of *Who Are My Parents?*[7]

Also young Mr. Fitzgerald believes in the literary gospel of St. Paul, and as such does not doubt that they have billed the Marion Davies screen classic in Minneapolis as "When Knighthood Was in Flour."[8]

---

[6] H. L. Mencken and George Jean Nathan, literary editors; Park & Tilford, whiskey manufacturer; Lord & Taylor, department store; Lea & Perrins, worcestershire-sauce producer; Smith Brothers, cough-drop manufacturer; and Mrs. Gibson, the pig lady, and her Jenny mule, figures in the sensational Hall-Mills murder case of 1922.

[7] Movie mogul William Fox was founder of Fox Films; the title of his 1922 silent film *A Little Child Shall Lead Them* was changed to *Who Are My Parents?* following a public competition allegedly won by a Bronx stenographer, Miss Julia Gordon.

[8] This joke about the 1922 Cosmopolitan/Paramount silent movie adapted from Charles Major's novel *When Knighthood Was in Flower* alludes to the fact that General Mills is located in Minneapolis, sister-city and rival of Fitzgerald's birthplace, St. Paul.

Is the Jelly Bean from Georgia?
Ward Greene / 1923

Reprinted from Fitzgerald's scrapbook.

Every time F. Scott Fitzgerald writes a story about the town of Tarleton, Ga. (he says in his last book, *Tales of the Jazz Age*), he gets an indignant letter from some sterling patriot, bitterly denouncing him as a traducer of the south.

Mr. Fitzgerald says he doesn't know why this should be so, as he actually loves and reveres the south and strives to picture it sympathetically. The writer is inclined to side with Mr. Fitzgerald in this. After reading his story of Tarleton's youth called "The Ice Palace," it is difficult to name any other writer who has so successfully caught and put on paper the serene beauty of slumbrous southern towns, the charm of their girls or the easy loveableness of their young men.

Still, just in case there are some resentful persons who believe Mr. Fitzgerald has painted Tarleton a bit too lazy and dreamful, let it be stated here and now that, when Fitzgerald describes Tarleton, he isn't describing a Georgia town at all; he is—Birmingham papers, please copy—talking about a place in Alabama!

This comes direct from Fitzgerald himself, via Messrs. Thomas Sherman and Floyd Traynham, two former southerners who are now editor and cameraman respectively for a big New York news reel company, and who went out to Long Island the other day to snap some movies of Mr. Fitzgerald and Mrs. Fitzgerald and the rest of the Fitzgerald family—a girl aged one.

"As a matter of fact, I never was in Georgia in my life," Mr. Fitzgerald told them, "except for a few weeks at Camp Gordon during the war. The rest of the time I was in the army I was stationed near Montgomery. When I write about the south, I write about it as I saw it in Alabama. I chose to use the name of Tarleton, Ga., because I know Georgia and Alabama towns are pretty much the same and because—well, just because I didn't want to get too specific. I don't know if this confession will rile Alabama or disappoint Georgia, or vice versa, but—it's true."

And then Mr. Fitzgerald went on to explain that, after he wrote his first story about Tarleton—I think it was "The Ice Palace," published in *Flappers and Philosophers*—he got such a budget of letters from sterling and indignant patriots of Ellijay, Monroe, Valdosta, Quitman, Moultrie, Marietta, Athens and other cities whose chambers of commerce thought Tarleton was their town, that he decided to switch locations.

So, when he wrote "The Jellybean" for the *Metropolitan* magazine, with a Tarletonesque hero and a drinking bee at the country club, he put this town in—Mississippi. And immediately the sterling patriots of Mississippi rose up and fell on him sword and buckler. So now, with "The Jellybean" republished in his new book, *Tales of the Jazz Age*, he's crossed out Mississippi and substituted Georgia again.

Does that mean he thinks Mississippians are worse tartars than Georgians? Or that Georgians are more appreciative of realism, even if it happens to be at their own expense?

I don't know. Perhaps, in his next Southern story, he will try Alabama, whence (he admits), he's really getting his inspiration.

Scott Fitzgerald, by all accounts, is a pretty likable chap for a young fellow who, before his twenty-fifth birthday, published two successful novels, two successful books of short stories and won the accolade of such critics as H. L. Mencken, Burton Rascoe and other frank speakers, who rank him high, if not first, among the younger American literati.

Rascoe has accused him of imitating James Branch Cabell. Fitzgerald laughs at this, for, as he says, he never heard of Cabell or of any other modern novelists until after he graduated from Princeton.

"Heaven knows I've imitated enough people he might have mentioned with some truth—Compton Mackenzie, for example," said Fitzgerald. (I think the Mackenzie comparison is apparent to anyone who has read *This Side of Paradise* and *Sinister Street*.)

Fitzgerald says he wrote and had rejected 144 short stories before he ever landed one. This sounds like the stock confession of every successful writer, but Fitzgerald swears it's true in his case.

This Side of Paradise was begun during the war, in which he served as a first lieutenant at southern camps. It was rejected by various publishers while he walked the streets of New York in search of a newspaper job which he never got. He went to his home in St. Paul, Minn., rewrote it, sent it to Harper's,[1] had it accepted, and immediately woke up to fame as a bestseller and to floods of requests for stories from magazine editors.

Mr. Fitzgerald married Zelda Sayre, of Montgomery. Since she has bobbed

---

[1] *This Side of Paradise* was published by Charles Scribner's Sons, not Harper and Brothers.

hair and is both beautiful and clever, she has been pointed out as the original of most of his heroines, including Gloria, of *The Beautiful and Damned*.

But Fitzgerald doesn't admit this. He says Mrs. Fitzgerald has been a great help to him—in fact, he acknowledges, in his foreword on "The Jellybean," his debt to her for the verisimilitude of the crap game in this story—but *The Beautiful and Damned*, he asserts, is more than the result of observation among his friends than it is autobiographical.

"I did," he confessed, "get a lot of material for this book and for *This Side of Paradise* from a diary of my wife's I found. Parts of it I ran without a cut or a change. But I've almost squeezed the book dry. I'll have to find some new material for my next novel."

He is working now on short stories. He is also preparing, with Mrs. Fitzgerald, a joint article for one of the national magazines.[2] She also writes, though she hasn't much time for it. The *Metropolitan* recently published her views on the flapper and the younger generation.[3]

The way Mr. Fitzgerald works is interesting. He doesn't use a typewriter—never did learn. He writes everything in longhand, edits it carefully, then writes it a second time.

He does not aspire to turn out quantity. He generally spends weeks on a single story, despite his boast in *Tales of the Jazz Age* that "The Camel's Back" was speeded out in twenty-four hours for the specific purpose of buying a piece of jewelry for his wife.

The Fitzgeralds, after living mostly in St. Paul since their marriage, have moved east permanently. They bought a home at Great Neck, Long Island,[4] where he will work henceforth.

According to my informants, the Boswell of the flapper is far from being the sophisticated, advanced, and cynical young man one might expect him to be. In fact, in his own home, he was domesticity itself.

The picture they draw of him is not of a long-haired aesthete, nor of a worldly-wise familiar of gin and petting parties, but of a clean-cut young husband and father who, instead of exploding "wise cracks" on life, spent most of their visit dancing up and down in front of his daughter, clapping his hands and making fatherly faces just like any ordinary mortal, in an effort to get her to smile for the cameraman.

---

[2] Possibly the brief essays, written by the Fitzgeralds and others, in response to the question "Does a Moment of Revolt Come Sometime to Every Married Man?" for *Mc-Calls* (March 1924).

[3] "Eulogy on the Flapper," June 1922.

[4] The Fitzgeralds rented a house at Great Neck; they never owned a home.

Novelist Flays Drys, Exalting Our Flappers

New York Daily News / 1923

F. Scott Fitzgerald, the young author who has achieved fame as the champion of the flapper both in fiction and in real life and whose great novel *The Beautiful and Damned* starts in the *Daily News* as a serial next Monday,[1] took a fling at prohibition yesterday in his home at Great Neck, L.I., where he lives with his wife, who was Zelda Sayre, and their baby.

The novelist was discussing the raid on Cushman's cabaret in Greenwich Village last Saturday night, when a score of flappers and young men were locked up and seven girls under twenty-one sent to the Florence Crittenton Home[2] by Magistrate Jean Norris.

"Prohibition is the cause of the conditions found in such places," said Fitzgerald. "Half the young people who get drunk or go to shady cabarets do so simply because prohibition has made an adventure instead of a disgrace of such parties.

"Say 'verboten' to youth and you challenge youth. When youth is challenged, it will make itself heard and felt, for in the end, youth is irrepressible. Those girls at Cushman's weren't vicious any more than the flappers in my novels are vicious.

"Why not raid the really nasty cabarets uptown? I've seen far more indecent dancing and drinking there and, for that matter, in the homes of our very best people, than ever took place in a Greenwich Village dance hall. Petting parties don't hurt a girl so much as a lot of reformers would have us believe."

---

[1] A cut version of the novel ran in the *Daily News* between 29 January and 26 March 1923.

[2] A New York City home for wayward girls.

Prediction Is Made about James Novel: F. S. Fitzgerald Believes *Ulysses* Is Great Book[1]

Richmond Times-Dispatch / 1923

Will James Joyce be to the next two generations what Henry James, Nietzsche, Wells, Shaw, Mencken, Dreiser, and Conrad have been to the present generation? F. Scott Fitzgerald, the prophet and voice of the younger American smart set, says that while Conrad's *Nostromo* is the great novel of the past fifty years, *Ulysses* by James Joyce, is the great novel of the future. In his list of "The Books I Have Enjoyed Most," Scott Fitzgerald places *A Portrait of the Artist as a Young Man* (Huebsch), as third from the top and avers that Joyce is to be "the most profound literary influence in the next fifty years."[2]

Whether the sons and daughters of the wild young things now who figure in Mr. Fitzgerald's brilliant pictures of the very present will actually read a great deal of Joyce we are left to guess, but the prediction which Mr. Fitzgerald makes of the intellectual temper of the new age may be a revelation to his many admirers. Fitzgerald stands today as a writer for and about the frivolous and semicynical. Samuel Butler, Friedrich Nietzsche and Anatole France were the intellectual influences which molded Fitzgerald's mind. He

---

[1] The headline writer confused James Joyce with Henry James.
[2] Fitzgerald's syndicated list included:
The Note-Books of Samuel Butler (1912), ed. Henry Festing Jones.
The Philosophy of Friedrich Nietzsche (1908), ed. H. L. Mencken.
A Portrait of the Artist as a Young Man (1916) and *Ulysses* (1922) by James Joyce.
Zuleika Dobson (1911) by Max Beerbohm.
The Mysterious Stranger (1916) by Mark Twain; ed. Albert Bigelow Paine and Frederick A. Duneka.
Nostromo (1904) by Joseph Conrad.
Vanity Fair (1847–48) by Thackeray.
The Oxford Book of English Verse (1921), ed. Arthur Quiller-Couch.
Thais (1890) by Anatole France.
Seventeen (1916) by Booth Tarkington.

says this in making up his list of books he enjoyed most. Ibsen and the Greek and Latin classics made Joyce, in a literary way, what he is. Is Joyce in turn to be the founder of a school of writers who will interpret the life of tomorrow with that same passionate naturalism, that amazing ability to depict "the stream of consciousness," the Gargantuan satire and laughter, and that unsentimental lyric joy in the unreserved acceptance of life, which distinguish Joyce's work as unique in this seething literary era?

What a "Flapper Novelist" Thinks of His Wife

The Courier-Journal / 1923

Reprinted from the *Courier-Journal* [Louisville], 30 September 1923, p. 112. Copyright © *Courier-Journal*. Reprinted by permission.

Is Zelda Sayre Fitzgerald, wife of Scott Fitzgerald, author of flapper fiction stories, the heroine of her husband's books? That's what a lot of "bestseller" patrons have been wondering.

If so, is she the living prototype of that species of femininity known as the American flapper? If so, what is a flapper like in real life? Here is a tabloid picture of Zelda Fitzgerald:

Flappers. She likes them reckless and unconventional, because of their quest in search of self-expression.

Sports. Golf and swimming.

Jazz music, "because it is artistic," and dancing for its sheer abandon. Not ambitious to be a "joiner"—just enjoy life to the full. Large families "so children have a chance to be what they want to be." Wants her own daughter to be "rich, happy and artistic."

If she had to earn her own living would go in for the ballet or the movies. Failing in that, she would try writing.

Home is the place to do what you like to do—not to live by the clock in a conventional way.

"So this is to be all about me?" asked Mrs. Scott Fitzgerald vivaciously. "I've never been interviewed before!"

She leaned far back into the plastic depths of an overstuffed chair, querying expectantly, "Now what do we do? Is it going to be very formal? Scott, please come into the living room and help me be interviewed."

Obediently Scott Fitzgerald left his study—scene of the creation of those brilliant tales to which American flappers thrill en masse. Tall, blond, broad-shouldered, he towers above his petite wife, whose blue eyes and yellow hair match his own.

"My stories?" Mrs. Fitzgerald said, "Oh, yes, I've written three. I mean, I'm writing them now. Heretofore, I've done several magazine articles. I like to write. Do you know, I thought my husband should write a perfectly good ending to one of the tales, and he wouldn't! He called them 'lop-sided,' too! Said that they began at the end."

She waved a gayly protesting white hand at her husband's efforts to explain that they were "good."

"Writing has its advantages," she continued. "Just think: I buy ever so many of Scott's presents that way. And buy ever so many other things on the theoretical proceeds of stories I'm going to write some day.

"Spending money is fun, isn't it?—Oh, yes, I wrote them in long hand. Typewriters are an unknown institution here at Great Neck."

Thus is necessitated the explanation that the abode of this charming and brilliant young couple among the newer lights of the modern literary world is a charming country house at Great Neck, Long Island.

Speaking "in domestic vein," which isn't the usual thing for her, Mrs. Fitzgerald remarked upon the absence of the butler. "He must be taking his saxophone lessons. Yes, today is the day. My great disappointment is that I've never heard him play; just infrequent tootings from afar.

"Yes. I love Scott's books and heroines. I like the ones that are like me! That's why I love Rosalind in *This Side of Paradise*. You see, I always read everything he writes. It spoils the fun, the surprise, I mean, a bit. Sometimes I act as official critic.

"But Rosalind! I like girls like that," she continued, shaking a curly crop of honey-yellow bobbed hair. "I like their courage, their recklessness and spendthriftness. Rosalind was the original American flapper.

"Three or four years ago girls of her type were pioneers. They did what they wanted to, were unconventional, perhaps, just because they wanted to for self-expression. Now they do it because it's the thing everyone does."

Asked to use his much-lauded gift for description in composing a word picture of his wife, he replied laconically and readily. "She is the most charming person in the world."

"Thank you, dear," was the gracious response.

Asked to continue the description thus commenced so auspiciously, he said: "That's all. I refuse to amplify. Excepting—she's perfect."

This last was given with an ardor worthy of one of his best heroes—Amory Blaine, for instance.

"But you don't think that," came the protest from the overstuffed arm chair. "You think I'm a lazy woman."

"No," judicially, "I like it. I think you're perfect. You're always ready to listen to my manuscripts at any hour of the day or night. You're charming—beautiful. You do, I believe, clean the ice box once a week."

"Oh, yes, I can draw. Scott says I don't know much about it, but that I draw well. And I play golf.

"I've a hearty liking for jazz music, especially Irving Berlin's," she continued. "It's most artistic. One of the first principles of dancing is abandon, and this is a quality that jazz music possesses. It's complex. It will, I believe, occupy a great place in American art."

At this juncture her husband decided to take a hand in the matter of interviewing. He propounded a series of questions with startling rapidity.

"Whom do you consider the most interesting character in fiction?"

After a considerable discussion no less a person than Becky Sharpe was decided upon.

"Only I do wish she'd been pretty," the interviewee said wistfully.

"What would your ideal day constitute?"

"Peaches for breakfast," was the prompt response. "There, that's a good start, isn't it? Let me see. Then golf. Then a swim. Then just being lazy. Not eating or reading, but being quiet and hearing pleasant sounds—rather a total vacuity. The evening? A large, brilliant gathering, I believe."

"Am I ambitious?" she echoed the next question. "Not especially, but I've plenty of hope. I don't want to belong to clubs. No committees. I'm not a 'joiner.' Just be myself and enjoy living."

"Do you like to study?"

This question asked, her husband eyed her merrily, as though expecting an outburst.

It was forthcoming.

"You know I don't. Never did. But my ancestors made up for any lack of brilliance of mine in that line."

"Do you like large or small families?"

"Large ones. Yes, quite large. The reason is that then children have a chance to be what they want to be—not oppressed by too much 'looking after,' nor influenced by ordinary life in any way.

"Children shouldn't bother their parents, nor parents their children. If possible to establish friendly relations, mutual understanding, between them, it's an excellent thing, but if this isn't possible, it seems worse to bring them together too much. Let children work out their own ideas as to duty to their parents, immortality and choosing a career."

"What do you want your daughter to do, Mrs. Fitzgerald, when she grows up?" Scott Fitzgerald inquired in his best reporterial manner, "not that you'll try to make her, of course, but—"

"Not great and serious and melancholy and inhospitable, but rich and happy and artistic. I don't mean that money means happiness, necessarily. But having things, just things, objects makes a woman happy. The right kind of perfume, the smart pair of shoes. They are great comforts to the feminine soul."

"What would you do if you had to earn your own living?" the catechism was continued.

"I've studied ballet. I'd try to get a place in the Follies. Or the movies. If I wasn't successful, I'd try to write."

Speaking of home life in general, and that of the Scott Fitzgeralds in particular, she declared that "Home is the place to do the things you want to do. Here, we eat just when we want to. Breakfast and luncheon are extremely movable feasts. It's terrible to allow conventional habits to gain a hold on a whole household; to eat, sleep and live by clock ticks."

Her favorite among her husband's writings are the episodes of Rosalind in *This Side of Paradise,* the last half of *The Beautiful and the Damned*, the short story, "The Off Shore Pirate" and the play, *The Vegetable.*

All of which leads to the conclusion that Zelda Sayre Fitzgerald, though by her own declaration "not ambitious," is responsible to no small degree for the remarkable success of her distinguished author-husband.

F. Scott Fitzgerald on "Minnie McGluke"

B. F. Wilson / 1923

Reprinted from *Picture-Play,* 19 (October 1923), pp. 83–84, 102.
Copyright © *Picture-Play.* Reprinted by permission.

The "spokesman for the younger generation," who is having quite a bit to do in connection with the movies these days, expresses himself freely and fearlessly on the making of them.

We were sitting in the cool of the enclosed porch. The most-talked-of-for-his-age author reclined at full length on a chaise-longue (we were so glad to see the latter, for the moment we espied it we knew we had the proper setting for our interview), while his fair young bride occupied a swinging divan with us. Something tinkled in tall glasses. A nurse introduced the two-year-old heiress of the Fitzgerald fortunes, and we immediately forgot the purpose of our visit in the enjoyment of infant beauty.

After a few moments of serious discussion on the phenomenal traits possessed by Miss Patricia Fitzgerald (answering, however, in the family circle to the more characteristic name of "Scotty"), we suggested the possibilities of this future beauty-contest winner taking up screen work as a career.

"Why not?" inquired the young father. "If she grows up to be a beauty, if she has any talent for motion-picture work, I shall certainly encourage her to take it up. I would never—if I could possibly avoid it—encourage her to go on the stage. I think the theatrical world a terrible place for a girl, but I think the life of the average intelligent movie star about as satisfactory as any. Certainly, to my mind, Mary Pickford[1] leads an existence envied, and quite rightly, too, by most women in the world. And besides, I think she is one of the very few great women we have. She has accomplished an enormous amount of work. She will, in all probability, remain a part of the history of this generation long after the names and deeds of most of the famous men will be forgotten."

---

[1] Silent screen actress known as "America's Sweetheart." She founded United Artists studio with Douglas Fairbanks, Charlie Chaplin, and D. W. Griffith.

We asked him if he shared the opinion of the sophisticated few about the movies.

"I quite frankly admit that I think they are usually terrible, but they're certainly here. Bernard Shaw once said that a cabinet minister who refused to 'recognize' a labor union always reminded him of a gondola refusing to recognize an ocean liner. As a writer, I feel that the movies are a tremendously important question."

He smiled a gay, young smile, which had something contagious about it.

"The movies remind me of the Triangle Club at Princeton. I used to belong to it, and we always started out firm in our decision to create new and startling things. We always ended up by producing the same old show. In the beginning, our enthusiasm and ideals discarded as rubbish all the old fossilized plots. We had everything in our favor to work with—our intentions to carry out new and brilliant plays were remarkable for their sincerity—and yet, every time the curtain went up there was the same old performance, differing by less than a hair from last year's show.

"Up till now, the movies have accomplished two wonderful things. The first is comedy—of course Charlie Chaplin is the most important product of the screen. His pictures are sophisticated and hilarious and have provided enough joy and laughter to make him immortal. Next, I think the picture of sheer action is far ahead of the serious picture. *The Covered Wagon* and *Tol'able David* were fine pictures.[2] They stuck closely to the original stories, they were simple, moving dramas of American life, and they have revealed a strange fact to hard-boiled motion-picture producers—that is, that a picture dealing with sex is so handicapped by the censorship that courage or revenge, which can be dealt with honestly, are now better movie themes than poor old 'ten-foot-kiss' love.

"It is amazing to me to see the stupidity and sheer ignorance of the average film producer. He has created for himself a mythical creature—half child, half woman, whose intelligence is just above that of an infant. This 'Minnie McGluke' stands for the audience to them who must be pleased and treated by and to pictures which only Minnie McGluke will care for. A producer shuns a story smacking of sincerity as he would the plague. He visualizes anything that makes the slightest departure from the usual hokum story, as being highbrow. 'Minnie' wouldn't understand such a picture—therefore it is not to be considered.

---

[2] *The Covered Wagon* (Famous Players-Lasky/Paramount, 1923) and *Tol'able David* (Inspiration Pictures/First National Exhibitors' Circuit, 1921).

"As a matter of fact, 'Minnie McGluke' is really a very small part of the movie audience. And even she enjoys just as much as anyone else a meritorious picture when she is given an opportunity to see one. How do you suppose pictures like *The Covered Wagon* and *Tol'able David* could make a million dollars for their creators if this were not true? How do you suppose *Robin Hood*[3] could succeed? Most of the men in power in filmdom have tentatively tried to meet the universal demand for 'better pictures' in the stupidest possible way. They spend a fortune on making a picture, the story of which has been written by some famous author. Usually the characters are 'society people'—the tremendous waste in trying to give convincing results by gorgeous gowns, exotic settings, et cetera, is almost laughable. They immediately get into the realm of pure fantasy. There is nothing intelligent about such productions—they are a silly exhibition of misplaced energy.

"And then when, quite naturally, not only 'Minnie' but everyone else views the super-special with a decided lack of enthusiasm, the producer decides that the public doesn't want anything highbrow—so back to the good old hokum—and that's what makes the rotten state of the movies prevail today."

"What do *you* think of that?" we demanded of the blond and beautiful better half of Mr. F. Scott Fitzgerald, who had been sitting quietly listening to her husband's tirade.

It is beyond us to reproduce the soft, delightful Southern drawl. We wish we could—for it is rarely heard in these tinny parts.

"Why, of course, I agree with everything he says," she smiled, "but, just the same, I go to the movies all the time. I am crazy about them, and although I do think most of the stories are simply terrible—I keep on going, and when I find a good one, I certainly do enjoy it."

"I am quite sure that the greatest fault lies in the fact that the writers of movie scenarios run to such extremes," continued Mr. Fitzgerald. "Why do they permit such terrible people to do the most important work? You remember the 'eminent authors' business developed at so much expense by Goldwyn.[4] You know what a fiasco it has turned out to be, because of the condescending attitude of the author. Most of the producers and most of the directors have since jumped to the conclusion that well-known writers are the

---

[3] Douglas Fairbanks Pictures Corporation/United Artists, 1922.
[4] Producer Samuel Goldwyn advertised that his movies were written by "eminent authors."

last people in the world fit to write stories for screening purposes. Do you know why? Many of the men with one or two exceptions, who were commissioned by Goldwyn to write scenarios had to take up the work at a rather late period of life. Such of them were pretty nearly old men, they had written straight narrative for many years, and now quite suddenly, they were to be able to create equally successfully in an entirely new field. There are a good many different angles which have to be taken into consideration in writing continuity. The absence of words makes it necessary to be able to render powerful dramatic impressions by visualizing.[5] This is extremely specialized habit of thought and, I believe, requires writing totally different from any other form in the world.

"If the producers, instead of turning back for relief to the most uninspired sort of hack writers, who with a few possible exceptions, have formerly limited their literary experience to press agenting, would take a few dozen of the younger good writers and first-rate newspapermen and try some such experiment as the eminent authors, I think it would undoubtedly lead to better stories being written for the movies. These younger men would learn the technique first of all; they would bring a freshness and enthusiasm to their work which has been lacking, and this, together with their creative ability, would certainly produce a far better method of obtaining good material than any method used up until now. Don't you agree with me?" he asked.

We certainly did and suggested that he try the idea out with some big film organization.

"I am doing something of this sort with Famous Players now," he replied. "They are going to produce *This Side of Paradise*, with Glenn Hunter in the title role.[6] I have written first of all a ten-thousand word condensation of my book. This is not a synopsis, but a variation of the story better suited for screening inasmuch as the book was a rambling, disconnected sort of thing, and had to be changed to fit the filming of it. After it has been O.K.'d, I shall work along with an experienced continuity writer on the scenario. This is a sort of experiment made by Famous Players, and I believe it is almost the first time anything of the kind has been done. I shall also have a hand in editing, titling and criticizing the picture—in short, I will be practically responsible for the whole story when it is finished with the exception of the actual shooting of the picture."

---

[5] Movies were silent before 1927.

[6] This movie was not made.

"Are you limiting your work now to the movies?" we asked.

"I should say not," replied this indolent-looking youth. "I have just finished an original story in which Glenn Hunter is working for the Film Guild. The name of it is *Grit*, and it has never been published. I wrote it for the Film Guild and Jim Creelman, one of the best continuity writers in the business revamped it, and they're filming it now.[7] My comedy, you know, *The Vegetable*, has been accepted for fall production by Sam Harris. That is my first play, and I am somewhat excited about its making a hit. Have you read it? Well, it is a queer thing, and I don't know just how it is going to go on the stage. I am also working on a novel—I think I have got hold of a very big idea, and I am very anxious to finish it. Outside of the play, the work for Famous, the novel and several orders for short stories, I haven't a thing to do at present."

---

[7] *Grit* was produced as "A heart-gripping, breathtaking melodrama of New York underworld" with Dore Davidson, Osgood Perkins, Roland Young, and Clara Bow.

F. Scott Fitzgerald Says: "All Women Over Thirty-five Should Be Murdered"

B. F. Wilson / 1923

Reprinted from *Metropolitan Magazine,* 58 (November 1923), pp. 34, 75–76. Copyright © *Metropolitan Magazine.* Reprinted by permission.

The press decries a superabundance and mushroom-growth of young intellectuals. A suffering public has had so many masterpieces of literature written by twenty-year-old hands of late that the age of our well-known authors is being carefully suppressed by wary publishers.

However, there are one or two exceptions where youth becomes a matter of minor importance. F. Scott Fitzgerald, author of *This Side of Paradise, The Beautiful and Damned, Tales of the Jazz Age,* etc., is a particularly noteworthy exception. Inasmuch as he is strictly responsible for the introduction into this country of a new and devastating type of girl whose movements, thoughts, and actions—to say nothing of deeds—have become matters of international importance, the editor decided that anything Mr. Fitzgerald might have to say on the subject of this department of the *Metropolitan Magazine* would be worth hearing.

So I hied myself down to Great Neck, Long Island. There in the cool of the afternoon, I visited with the famous young author and his family.

He made me feel completely at home from the moment I entered the house. He had just awakened from a nap and I caught him as he came into the library to fetch a book. A quiet dressing-gown covered a more distracting pair of pajamas. His blond hair was tousled like the head of a sleepy kid, and he seemed a bit nonplussed at my somewhat abrupt appearance.

He called loudly for the bride. Parking me with the comic supplement of the Sunday paper, he disappeared into the upper regions of the house. When he reentered the library he was clad in the conventional knickerbockers of the country gentleman; but the tousled-hair boy was still there.

"Didn't you feel desperate when you saw the result of your handiwork?" I asked him. "And aren't you glad that the flapper craze is passing?"

"But I don't think it is," he protested. "The flapper is going stronger than ever; she gets wilder all the time. She keeps on doing the things she has done before, and adding to them all the time. She is continuously seeking for something new to increase her store of experience. She still is looking for new conventions to break—for new thrills, for sensations to add zest to life, and she is growing more and more terrible."

"You know we've often wondered how she came into existence," I interrupted. "Just how she arrived and where from. Quite a few people attribute her to you. They claim she sprang from your books and stories. Is it true?"

He smiled a bit ruefully.

"Did you ever read Thackeray's *Henry Esmond*?" he asked. "Well, Beatrice was the first flapper. She lived for thrills; she turned over two kingdoms to indulge a whim and to see just how much power she possessed over the Young Pretender. She lived to embroil herself in one intrigue after another. Sensation was the breath of life to her, and inasmuch as the ladies of her century were still in the obscure stage of subservience to the male, she was a distinct shock to the middle classes and the court reporter.

"She was the first woman to test openly her power over men. She was the first to manifest a desire for independence.

"Much later, the suffragette type came into existence. You know how she clamored for independence. She was a horrible person. A woman of thwarted desires endeavoring to satisfy her restlessness by demanding from men that which they had refused to surrender by persuasion. She couldn't attract men; therefore she decided to fight them."

He ran restless fingers through his hair as he warmed to his subject.

"Just before the war, a new type of girl had appeared in England. You remember Stephen McKenna's books,[1] don't you? Well, most of his heroines were flappers. Then there was an outbreak of new heroines in English life and letters. They wanted independence. They loved danger and were excitement-mad and faintly neurotic. They realized that men were adamant to the suffragette type; therefore, they stopped bombing Prime Ministers. But they showed their independent spirit in other ways. They discussed subjects which had hitherto been considered taboo for women; they lived independently of their families; they were to be seen everywhere unchaperoned. In short, having decided that unto each person life was an individual law, they did as they pleased. When their actions began to arouse comment, they increased their daring.

---

[1] The novels of this prolific English author included *Lady Lilith* (1921) and *The Secret Victory* (1921).

"When the war came on they had a new outlet for their energy. Of course by this time, this type had drifted into America. I had no idea of originating an American flapper when I first began to write. I simply took girls whom I knew very well and, because they interested me as unique human beings, I used them for my heroines.

"I lived out West. In Chicago and St. Paul, for instance, the girls of my acquaintance seemed utterly different from any girls I had ever read about. Of course money was the direct reason. In the Middle West there was wealth without background, tradition, or manners, in the broad sense of the word. Naturally, with this new and powerful resource in their hands to do with as they desired, many of the younger girls could use their leisure and exuberant vitality only in some form of excess.

"Then Freud came into existence. He has had the widest influence on the younger generation. You cannot begin to conceive how far his theories have spread in America. I remember a girl—one of the nicest girls I ever knew. She had never heard of Freud, but she had begun to ask questions. We talked one evening, and she informed me that whether by hearing other girls talk, or by analyzing her own unhappiness, she had discovered herself to be a victim of suppressed instinct."

He waved his hand in an emphatic gesture.

"Why, Freud at third-hand ran over this country like wildfire. He gave the wealthy young girls something new in the way of sensationalism. They decided that they were all victims of repressed desires, and began to cut loose. When the war was over and the young men came back, the best and smartest of them disillusioned at the fiasco of their ideals, they subconsciously helped the independence of the girls along."

"Well, don't you think the young girl of today is beginning to tire of all this sensationalism?" I asked.

"Not at all," he replied emphatically. "I think she is going on and on, carrying the younger men with her—until there will be some sort of catastrophe which may or may not face her in another direction. Look at all the unhappy girls you see—look at the number of wretched marriages. Look at the increase in divorce—look at the increase in extra-nuptial affairs. Of course she is an awe-inspiring young person. I thoroughly dislike her as a rule—unless she is very pretty and has authentic charm—or on the other hand, unless she is intelligent enough to conduct herself with sense and discretion. Most of them are so messy with their amours."

He smiled at his own intensity of feeling—but we knew he meant what he said.

"By 1915, the best send-off a girl who visited in St. Paul could possibly have was that she bore the reputation of being a violent petter, and had driven innumerable men to distraction. And, as I have said before, I think she is growing wilder all the time."

He looked me straight in the eye.

"Be perfectly frank, now," he said. "Don't you think men are much nicer than women? Don't you find them more open and aboveboard, more truthful and more sincere? Wouldn't you a whole lot rather be with a bunch of men than with a group of women?"

I had to confess to the impeachment.

"I know that after a few moments of inane conversation with most girls I get so bored that unless I have a few drinks I have to leave the room."

As if in answer to his argument, a beautiful young woman appeared in the doorway. Instantly a wide smile lit up his features. He introduced me to his wife.

"Zelda," he explained. "I was on my customary thesis of the superiority of men over women." He turned towards me. "She agrees with me entirely. We always have the house full of my friends, and when I ask her if she wouldn't like to have some girls down for a weekend she declines with thanks."

"Why, Scotty, aren't you horrid?" she protested in a soft Southern drawl. "You know I have a lot of girls down here all the time. But just the same, I must admit," she confessed smiling to me, "that I have a better time when Scotty's friends are here.

"He's just a crank on the subject of women," she continued. "He says that all women over thirty-five should be murdered."

The husband protested.

"I mean the women who, without any of the prerogatives of youth and beauty, demand continual slavery from their men," he said warmly. "You know the type. There are thousands of them. They sit back complacently and watch their husbands slave for them; and, without furnishing any of the pleasantries of life for their husbands, they demand the sort of continual attention that a charming fiancée might get. They make tame-cats of them. They are harridans and shrews who continually nag and scold until the men are driven idiotic.

"I have one of them in my new play, *The Vegetable*. Of course she isn't as fully developed as the kind I mean, but you would know her instantly."

As I left the house I carried with me a rather pleasant picture. As handsome a young author as I ever hope to see, this F. Scott Fitzgerald of twenty-five or six. As pretty a young wife as rarely falls to the lot of any man. And last, but first in importance to these two, as lovely a two-year-old female answering to the name of "Scotty" as ever beamed on a wonderful world.

Notes on Personalities, IV—F. Scott Fitzgerald

B. F. Wilson / 1924

Reprinted from the *Smart Set,* 73 (April 1924), pp. 29–33. Copyright
© *The Smart Set.* Reprinted by permission.

The strange attraction that a pool of quiet waters has for the boy or man with
a stone in his hand is largely a matter of personal curiosity. How far will the
ever-widening circles of water spread? What happens when the last wave
breaks upon the bank is of no interest to him: his attention is concentrated
upon his own reaction to the disturbance of nature's serenity by his ability to
hurl a stone.

This is the story of a boy who, some five years ago, threw a rock into the
placid waters of American literature with such force that the splash was heard
all over the country, and the waves are still crashing into larger convolutions,
bringing in their wake strange matters which continue to absorb the interest
of the world at large.

Francis Scott Fitzgerald was the first author to chronicle the younger generation at the moment when youth was becoming supreme and defiant. Pubes-
cence had mushroomed overnight into a powerful factor of every-day
existence. A new era was dawning. A new type of girl was being created.

This was the beginning of the Flapper Age, an epoch during which the
heroine of *This Side of Paradise* exerted a drastic influence. Her actions, her
speech, her manners, her habits and her appearance were under the micro-
scope, and she permeated every phase of life from the schoolroom to politics.

When it was learned that the author of *This Side of Paradise* was a young
man in the first year of voting possibility, the amazement of the reading
public turned into something like frenzy. The book became a bestseller in
two weeks. Critics raved over the discovery of a new literary personality.
Their blurbs on the merits and the depravity of the book were taking up all
the space in the daily press. F. Scott Fitzgerald's became a household name;
débutantes dreamed on it, hard-boiled critics foamed at the mouth, college
youths and faculty members quarreled, mothers sighed, fathers wept, shop-
girls envied and country wenches patterned their conduct along the lines

exampled by the heroine of the story—in short, something more than a stir
was made by the appearance of this incoherent, disconnected, flagellating,
first novel which sold into the hundred thousand copies.

Various and contradictory personality paragraphs about the author appeared before the public in every sort of pamphlet. He was an old man; he
was a young *roué;* he was a typical Westerner who wore a big sombrero; he
was a college youth who wrote only when completely spifflicated on absinthe
and gin. He was a bad moral influence for the country. But the wise men of
letters sat back and predicted fine things of this infant-in-quills.

Scott Fitzgerald admits them to be right. He is intensely egotistical, but it
is the same egotism that a precocious youngster shows to an admiring group
of adults. Even as the youngster with smug satisfaction recites his little piece,
his tongue in his cheek, so does the blond-haired, blue-eyed historian of the
Flapper drive his pen over the blank page. . . .

He has set forth, for instance, in his writing that all the great heroes of the
world had blue eyes and yellow hair (as he himself has). It is logical hence
to expect the unusual when one meets this good-looking young man. He is
vivacious, imaginative, forceful—and slightly unbalanced. The latter is his
chief charm. It reveals itself in impulses which would never occur to a more
prosaic soul, in his daydreams, in his worship of the beautiful, and in his
creation of characters who linger in one's memory.

He is an actor. The dramatic instinct has been a large part of his character
ever since he was a little boy. This trait, intensified by his soaring imagination, is the backbone of his work.

F. Scott Fitzgerald was born in 1896 and was christened for his famous
ancestor who wrote our national anthem. His father, a heady young South-
erner, followed Greeley's advice and found himself in Minnesota when
scarcely more than a boy, penniless but hopeful, and in love with the daughter
of a wealthy wholesale grocer. Since this was the age of optimism, the couple
married, and for the first twelve years of his life the future novelist lived in
St. Paul,[1] as one of the most widely-discussed show pieces of that city. He
had to sing and recite to his mother's guests, and in addition it became noised
about that he had written a story at seven, and at ten had begun a history of
the United States.

His first tragedy occurred when he was six years old, and the episode left

[1] Fitzgerald was born in St. Paul but lived in upstate New York between April 1898 and
July 1908.

a wound which he will never forget. He was giving his first birthday party. The dramatic instinct soared as he saw himself clad in his long-trousered sailor suit assuming the role of host. For weeks he had been revelling in anticipation. It was to mark his formal entrance into society, and he kept meticulous watch over his attire during the hours he had to wait before the party would begin. It started to rain. Nobody came. All the long afternoon he waited silently, and when the rain stopped and the sun came out, he stood on the porch of the house still hoping that the children would arrive. No one came, and finally dusk fell. He went into the house and at the sight of the birthday cake and other refreshments his heart almost broke.

At school he wanted to lead all activities. Unless he was permitted to start the games and was chosen as leader, he was unhappy. This trait is not a very popular one amongst schoolboys unless the desire is reinforced by brute strength, and Scott was a delicate child. Consequently he was unpopular, and on one occasion he was told to "go away," that "he wasn't wanted." The boy's egotistic nature suffered deeply. Furthermore, he had a habit of writing all through class in the back of his geography book, or Latin, or mathematical books. This added to his unpopularity because the boys couldn't understand his absorption. As a result of the eternal scribbling, his studies fell short of parental expectations, and he was sent away to boarding school.

From his earliest memory Scott Fitzgerald suffered from a pedentia complex. The sight of his own feet filled him with embarrassment and horror. No amount of persuasion could entice him to permit others to see his naked feet, and up until he was twelve this fear caused him a great deal of misery. He refused to learn how to swim. His family accused him of being afraid of the water, but although he endured agony at being called various names which implied lack of courage—he refused to go into the water. He loved the sea, and pleaded that he be allowed to wear his stockings swimming. This complex suddenly disappeared one day without any reason.

When he was eleven he had his first short story published in *Now and Then*, the school organ of the St. Paul Academy. It was called "The Mystery of the Raymond Mortgage." The mortgage in question was mentioned exactly twice in the story: in the title and again in the second paragraph, after which the young author became so engrossed in a lurid murder which one of his characters had committed that the mystery mentioned was never solved.

A year later he wrote "Elavo," a novel in verse, dealing with knights of old, Roman strongholds, drawbridges, et cetera. School requirements at the time included the reading of Walter Scott! It was during this period of his life that he obtained the only historical education he has ever retained. An Aunt Clara, whom he visited during vacations in New Hampshire, was firmly convinced that her nephew was not long for this world, and that the best way he could strengthen his hold on life was to swallow one raw egg every day. To enforce this she bribed him with a twenty-five-cent piece for each egg he could keep down, and when he discovered that with this hard-earned wealth he could purchase a volume of Henty,[2] his distaste for the egg vanished. Each day he would rush down to the local bookshop with his quarter and by night the volume would be finished. . . .

The entire city of St. Paul was thrown into hysterical confusion not long after this by the appearance of a new dramatic genius. A lurid drama, entitled *The Captured Shadow*, was presented at a local theatre. The members of the cast were rather young, but so was the author. He was fifteen, and never before had an audience been privileged to witness such a mixture of all the old familiar thrillers. The jokes were pilfered outright from a joke book. The hero, who naturally was played by Scott Fitzgerald, inasmuch as he wrote the drama, drew great applause as he gracefully swooned into the heroine's arms before the final curtain.

But in boarding school he went off on a new tack. He saw a musical comedy called *The Quaker Girl*, and from then on he filled dozens of notebooks with librettos modeled after Gilbert and Sullivan. He discovered that the only collegiate musical comedy flourished at Princeton, and on this information he made his choice of where he was to go to college.

He fell down on his studies during his freshman year, but he wrote an operetta for the Triangle Club. The play was accepted and produced, and Scott caused great excitement as the most beautiful of the chorus girls.

This aptitude for female impersonation caused a furor at a prom at the University of Minnesota, where one evening appeared an unknown and beautiful young woman. She shocked her dancing partners by guzzling drinks and smoking fiercely, and in addition threw confusion into the host of collegiate youths who had surrounded her in admiration, by playing one of them against the other. After securing written evidence of ardent admiration from some of the most popular boys, she suddenly disappeared, like Cinderella at midnight, and for days the mystery was the choicest bit of discussion in St. Paul.

In the autumn of 1916–17 he embarked for an infantry officers' training camp at Fort Leavenworth—the poetry which he had been furiously writing

---

[2] G. A. Henty, prolific English author of boys' books.

for some time past in the discard—with a new ambition. This time it was to be the Great American Novel and accordingly every evening, concealing his pad behind his Small Problems for Infantry, he wrote a sort of biographical story of himself and what life meant to him. Despite the fact that this little game was detected and stopped, his burning ambition to finish the novel before he departed for Europe drove him to the Officers' Club, and every Saturday at one o'clock he sat down to his task in a corner of a roomful of smoke, conversation and a thousand and one interruptions from facetious fellow officers. Stimulated by innumerable drinks of Coca-Cola, he wrote one hundred and twenty thousand words during the week-ends of the next three months. The book was aptly enough titled by the author "The Romantic Egotist" and sent to a publisher's. It was returned with a long letter stating that while the manuscript was the most original received for years, the firm could not publish it. It was too crude and incoherent.

Scott never got overseas. Some six months afterward he came to New York, in the meanwhile having fallen madly in love and become betrothed to Zelda Sayre, a brilliant and beautiful Southern girl whom he met while at camp in Alabama.

He had to make money. But how? He tried to get a job as a newspaper reporter, but no one wanted him. Finally he went to work for Barron Collier, writing advertising copy during the day, and after office hours working on short stories. They were all returned. He made for himself a beautiful frieze which ran around his room out of the one hundred and twenty-two rejection slips which he received from editors. He wrote movies. Song lyrics. Complicated advertising schemes. Poems. Sketches. Jokes. No one bought them. Near the end of June he sold a story for thirty dollars.

The ninety dollars a month which he was earning seemed too silly to waste anymore time over, and besides, love was clamoring for recognition. So Scott decided to take a drastic step. He gave up his job, packed his bag and went back to St. Paul. There he announced to a somewhat surprised family that he had come home to write a novel. They took it with as little display of commiseration as possible.

In the next two hot months he sat steadily before his desk, revising, compiling and boiling down "The Romantic Egotist." He changed the title to "This Side of Paradise." It was accepted by special delivery. In the next two months he wrote eight short stories and sold nine. The ninth was accepted by the same magazine that had rejected it four months before. After the appearance of the novel he got married and brought his bride East. . . .

Now they live down at Great Neck, Long Island, where the sovereign of the family is a two-year-old female answering to the name of "Scotty," despite the fact that she had been christened Patricia. Mrs. Fitzgerald writes also. She has a queer, decadent style, luminous in its imagination, and very often Scott incorporates whole chapters of his wife's writing into his own books.[3] He steals all of her ideas for short stories and writes them as his own.

He is at present working on a novel. He wants to write a musical comedy and a play. He utters sentiments like this:

"When I was twenty I wanted to be King of the World, a sort of combined J. P. Morgan, General Ludendorff, Abraham Lincoln, and Nietzsche not to omit Shakespeare." There he stops. There is an implication that he has hopes of being all this still.

"I would like to have an awful lot of money with which to buy all the books I want and a Rolls Royce car."

"I'd like to spend eight months in travel, and have four children. They are cheerful, decorative and amusing to have around the house."

"I'd like to go into politics."

"I am glad I'm a young man in America now."

"I'd like to spend eight months in England during the Regency period. Life was so riotous and colorful and gay then. It was the last of the powder and patch days, and the great spirits like Johnson and Byron were casual figures on the street.[4] Also it was beginning to be possible then for a man to earn his living with his pen."

"And I'd like to have been a young Englishman during the first decade of the present century. The Fabian Society was getting on its feet. Oxford and Cambridge were turning out interesting men, and the inhibitions of the Victorian era were passing away. I would hate to have been a young man between the accession of Victoria and her death."

"I'd like to have been a young Spaniard about 1550 in the glory of the Armada. I would hate to have been a Roman or a Greek of any period. I would like to have been a young Venetian when Venice was the thoroughfare of the civilized world and all the crusaders passed through her gates."

"My heroes? Well, I consider H. L. Mencken and Theodore Dreiser the greatest men living in the country today."

---

[3] Untrue. Fitzgerald was joking if he said this to the reporter.

[4] Samuel Johnson (1709–1784) and Lord Byron (1788–1824) could not have been in London at the same time.

His imagination is the predominant power behind Scott Fitzgerald's pen. He gloats over a good simile as a woman would over a priceless jewel. He loves to roll gorgeous phrases on his tongue. His delight in the beauty of words is sensuous.

He is left-handed,[5] and his chirography is that of a small schoolboy.

He is an earnest worker and when occupied in writing refuses to play. Although he is a boon companion he cannot escape from his thoughts, and in order to avoid hearing the telephone, encountering people, or listening to the every-day noises of his household, he has fitted a room over his garage and daily spends most of the waking hours in hard toil.

---

[5] Fitzgerald wrote with his right hand, though he did everything else with his left.

F. Scott Fitzgerald[1]

Charles C. Baldwin / 1924

Reprinted from Charles C. Baldwin, *The Men Who Make Our Novels* (New York: Dodd, Mead, 1924), pp. 166–73. Copyright © Dodd, Mead. Reprinted by permission.

If I were given to prophecying I should certainly predict, once his mania for writing ephemeral short stories is done with, a great and glorious future for F. Scott Fitzgerald; and I should base that prediction upon the irony, the beauty, the wit of *This Side of Paradise* and *The Beautiful and Damned*. There are two books unique in American literature, though imitated a thousand times. They are the young man sowing his oats, reaping his whirlwind, muddled, worried, triumphant and moody, with his gay colors and gray castles tumbled in a heap. They have form, ease and variety. They are utterly fearless, shirking no conclusions, true to their characters.

If a chap is a bounder, selfish and conceited, soon or late his friends will find it out. Fitzgerald knows this. But that does not blind him to the fact that the chap may be immensely interesting and, in his way, tragic and likable. The chap may be generous; the cad may be a pose—as it was with Byron. Or the loss may be a woman's, some woman who has put her trust in him. But not always. Sometimes the loss is ours. If I remember right, Sidney Carton was a sot, but his is the only name one regrets and recalls when *A Tale of Two Cities* is done with—as, in the course of the years, most books are done with, becoming only memories half and more than half forgotten.

But it is not so much his characters that matter, to Fitzgerald and in his books, as what is done with them. In *This Side of Paradise* they are given their heads, in *The Beautiful and Damned* rope. Yet when they threaten to run away or hang themselves, Fitzgerald does not wring his hands and say, "I told you so." Nor does he stand idly by and shrug his shoulders, murmuring, "The funeral is theirs." He lets them play their piece out to the end; and they become, even for the dullest, tragic comedians, dangling helplessly on

---

[1] This article incorporates material from Fitzgerald's undated letter to Baldwin; see *Trimalchio* (Columbia: University of South Carolina Press in Cooperation with the Thomas Cooper Library, 2000), Postscript.

the threads of destiny and time. Rightly understood, they are heroic—and Fitzgerald understands them absolutely.

"My third novel," he says, "is just finished and quite different from the other two in that it is an attempt at form and refrains carefully from trying to 'hit anything off.' Five years ago the new American novels needed comment by the author because they were facing a public that had had very little but trash for a hundred years—that is to say, the exceptions were few and far between and most of them were commercial failures. But now that there is an intelligent body of opinion guided by such men as Mencken, Edmund Wilson, and Van Wyck Brooks, comment should be unnecessary; and the writer, if he has any aspirations toward art, should try to convey the feel of his scenes, places and people directly—as Conrad does, as a few Americans (notably Willa Cather) are already trying to do."

Mr. Fitzgerald was born in St. Paul, Minn., Sept. 24, 1896. He spent his early years traveling with his family here and there through America, living for a while in Syracuse and for a while in Buffalo. His first reading was entirely confined to Henty, Alger, and Ralph Henry Barbour.[2] At college he was influenced, almost exclusively, by Wells and Compton Mackenzie—as he says, "see *This Side of Paradise* which treats all this very fully, being to a large extent autobiographical."

That incorrigible gossip, Burton Rascoe, in the *New York Tribune*, tells of a luncheon with Edmund Wilson during which Wilson remarked that Fitzgerald mispronounces more words than any other educated person he (Wilson) has ever known; going on to say that when Fitzgerald is with Ring Lardner, Lardner is forever correcting Fitzgerald's pronunciation. However, no harm is done as Fitzgerald never remembers the correction from one moment to the next.

Among other wise sayings Ed Howe[3] has said that somehow we always hate to tell a man that he can't spell. Spelling, nevertheless, is a part of writing. The history of a word is in its spelling—whence it hails and who has used it, Latin or Greek or Teuton, and where, under what moon, across what council table, for whose ears. This is my only excuse for referring to the spelling of Fitzgerald in a recent letter to me. . . .

Fitzgerald is free from all feeling for words. He uses them or abuses them

---

[2] Along with Henty, Horatio Alger and Ralph Henry Barbour were prolific authors of popular books for boys.

[3] E. W. Howe, newspaper editor and author of *The Story of a Country Town* (1883).

as suits his fancy. He coins them anew. They are divorced from their past, made over, becoming utterly modern tramps as are so many of Fitzgerald's best-liked characters, and somehow individual—awhile, Ralph Henry Barber, Sarycuse, Compton Mackenzie, Van Wyke Brooks, Nietchean, Gertrude Stien, traveling. . . .

But don't let that worry you: the man's an artist just the same.

"When, in St. Paul and about twelve," says Fitzgerald, "I wrote all through class in school in the back of my geography and first year Latin and on the margin of themes, declensions, and mathematic problems. Two years later the family decided the only way to force me to study was to send me to a boarding school. This was a mistake. It took my mind off my writing. I decided to play football, to smoke, to go to college, to do all sorts of irrelevant things that had nothing to do with the proper mixture of description and dialogue in the short story.

"But in school I went off on a new tack. I saw a musical comedy called *The Quaker Girl* and from that day forth my desk bulged with Gilbert and Sullivan librettos and dozens of notebooks containing the germs of dozens of musical comedies.

"Near the end of my last school year I came across a musical comedy score lying on top of the piano. It was a show called *His Honor the Sultan* presented by the Triangle Club of Princeton University. That was enough for me. The University question was settled. I was bound for Princeton.

"I spent my entire freshman year writing an operetta for the Triangle Club. I failed in algebra, trigonometry, coordinate geometry and hygiene, but the Triangle Club accepted my show, and by tutoring all through a stuffy August I managed to come back a sophomore and act in it as a chorus girl.[4] A little later I left college to spend the rest of the year recuperating in the West.

"The next year, 1916–17, found me back in college, but by this time I had decided that poetry was the only thing, so with my head ringing with the meters of Swinburne and the matters of Rupert Brooke, I spent the spring doing sonnets, ballads, and rondels. I had read somewhere that every great poet had written great poetry before he was twenty-one. I had only a year and, besides, war was impending. I must publish a book of startling verse before I was engulfed.

---

[4] Fitzgerald did not perform in any of his Triangle Club shows because of academic probation. However, a photograph of him dressed as a showgirl apeared in the Rotogravure section of the 2 January 1916 *New York Times*.

"By autumn I was in an infantry officer's training camp with poetry in the discard and a brand new ambition—I was writing an immoral[5] novel. Every evening, concealing my pad behind Small Problems for Infantry, I wrote on a somewhat edited history of me and my imagination. And then I was detected and the game was up. I could write no more during study period.

"This was a distinct complication. I had only three months to live—in those days all infantry officers thought they had only three months to live—and I had left no mark in the world. But such consuming ambition was not to be thwarted. Every Saturday at one o'clock I hurried up to the Officer's Club, and there, in a corner of a room full of smoke, conversation and rattling newspapers, I wrote a one-hundred-and-twenty-thousand word novel on the consecutive weekends of three months. There was no revising; there was no time for it. As I finished each chapter I sent it to a typist in Princeton.

"I went to my regiment happy. I had written a novel. The war could now go on. I forgot paragraphs and pentameters, similes and syllogisms. I got to be a first lieutenant, got my orders over seas—then the publishers wrote that though 'The Romantic Egoist' was original they could not publish it. Six months after this I arrived in New York and presented my card to the office boys of seven city editors asking to be taken on as a reporter. I had just turned twenty-two, the war was over, and I was going to trail murderers by day and do short stories by night. But the newspapers sent their office boys out to tell me they didn't need me. They decided definitely and irrevocably by the sound of my name on a calling card that I was absolutely unfitted for a reporter. Instead I became an advertising man at ninety dollars a month, writing the slogans that while away the weary hours in rural trolley cars. After hours I wrote stories—from March to June. There were nineteen all together; the quickest written in an hour and a half, the slowest in three days. No one bought them, no one sent personal letters. I had one hundred and twenty-two rejection slips pinned in a frieze about my room. I wrote movies. I wrote song lyrics. I wrote complicated advertisement schemes, I wrote poems, I wrote sketches. I wrote jokes. Near the end of June I sold one story for thirty dollars.

"On the Fourth of July, utterly disgusted with myself and all the editors, I went to St. Paul and informed family and friends that I had given up my position and had come home to write a novel. They nodded politely, changed the subject, and spoke of me very gently. By this time I knew that I had a

---

[5] Thus in the interview, but Fitzgerald almost certainly said *immortal*.

novel to write, and all through two hot months I wrote and revised and compiled and boiled down. On September 15 *This Side of Paradise* was accepted by special delivery.

"In the next two months I wrote eight stories and sold nine. The ninth story was accepted by the same magazine that had rejected it four months before. In November, I sold my first story to the *Saturday Evening Post*. By February I had sold them half a dozen. Then my novel came out. Then I got married. Then I wrote *The Beautiful and Damned.* Now I spend my time wondering how it all happened."

"I am a pessimist, a communist (with Nietzschean overtones), have no hobbies except conversation—and I am trying to repress that. My enthusiasms at present include Stravinsky, Otto Braun,[6] Mencken, Conrad, Joyce, the early Gertrude Stein, Chaplin and all books about that period which lies between the V and XV centuries."

---

[6] *The Diary of Otto Braun* (1924)—a young German writer killed in the Battle of the Argonne—was greatly admired by Fitzgerald.

Un Giovane Autore Americano[1]

V. R. / 1925

Labeled in Fitzgerald's hand as from *Cosmopolis* (Rome), February 1925. Reprinted from Fitzgerald's scrapbook. Translated by Fausto Pauluzzi.

Hardly anyone knows him in Italy. In America, his name is very well known in all cities where literature matters the most. A friend who acts as the spiritual go-between for foreign *literati* passing through our city introduced me to him. I went to see him in his apartment in Piazza di Spagna and I found him focused on recording on paper some pencil notations: his impressions of Rome. Mr. Gerald, inwardly focused on the passion for his art, has come to Italy to give the last touches to a new novel, which is fruit of his deep psychological study of the sensitivity and liveliness of our Latin character. He lets no one force the secret of his work in progress; with the rude and jovial frankness that distinguishes the ultramodern people of which he's part, he forbade me categorically to ask him anything about its topic. I resigned myself, therefore, to recording his thoughts on the present situation of contemporary American literature.

—It is said that in America many of the better young authors have devoted themselves significantly to writing novels and short stories for the cinema: either because the attraction of money has prevailed on their passion for art, or because they receive immediate and greater moral satisfaction.

—Not at all, not at all . . . Mr. Gerald interrupted me, I'm well aware that abroad you have not so comforting an idea of our literature, but it's not really so. You have to make distinctions. I, for example, and many others with me, have never let a work be adapted and reconstructed for use in film—and never will.[2] The day I would decide to let it happen, I'd no longer belong to the grouping of pure men of letters. I would be listed among movie company clerks, who are pressured to adjust their brains and imagination to the artistic fickleness of the boss, who in turn chooses the story, the characters, and the

---

[1] "A Young American Author"

[2] Untrue. Fitzgerald's first three novels and several of his short stories were adapted for the movies during his lifetime.

duration of the action. Besides, of course, requiring a heavy dose of maudlin sentimentality between the leading young actress and Mr. X or Y.

And at this point Mr. Gerald wanted to update me minutely on the bitter and tenacious struggle that the major exponents of American literature have taken up against these manufacturers of film stories.

From his clearly reflected thoughts, I was able to gather how pure literary art is threatened by this damaging phenomenon in all countries where the movie industry has a solid base. In my opinion, though, the process of selection that involves authors of literary art and authors of film stories is taking care of things on its own. This is evidenced by the fact that the success of a film—even when we grant that film-story writing involves intelligence—is tied to the ability of a director.

We must not ignore that the development and growth of motion picture making might harm literature in general. However, in America they have started veritable crusades against those "clerks of the pen" who, on the whole, have curtailed their literary careers in the belief that with film-story writing they would achieve glory before others, with less effort. Too late did they realize that their genius was being disgracefully exploited by film companies who tied their own names to raging successes—while giving no credit to scriptwriters.

America has an abundance of such young writers, whereas its true men of letters are few. The latter are influenced by the realist short story writer Theodore Driesen and by the critic Menken.[3]

A short story by Sinclair Lewis, "Wall Street,"[4] in which the writer analyses social life in a small American city, and "The Three Soldiers" by John dos Passos, a Portuguese-American author who with refined irony lashes at the instigators of American intervention in the past World War—these have achieved unprecedented literary success thanks to the criticism of Menken.

In the field of theater, George Jean Nathan, a critic of unmistakable worth, by introducing the work of two illustrious foreign writers, Pirandello and Molnar,[5] has been able to cleanse the American stage of plays filled with that sad and banal sentimentalism that had been afflicting legitimate theater.

---

[3] Presumably the reputations of Theodore Dreiser and H. L. Mencken had not reached Italy at this time.

[4] *Main Street* (1920). In *Tender Is the Night* Dick Diver reads an Italian newspaper reference to Lewis's "Wall Street."

[5] Italian playwright Luigi Pirandello (1867–1936) and Hungarian playwright Ferenc Molnár (1878–1952).

But the most interesting and encouraging event to note is the success achieved by a recent American publication, *American Mercury,* directed by the most worthwhile of the critics among.[6] . . .

Those who follow with great interest the slow but sure rebirth of American literature should get to know that publication. They will agree that its pages present a healthy and intelligent literary criticism that offers a more honest and enjoyable evaluation of literary and theater pieces from America and Europe.

---

[6] The sentence is broken in the original text.

Ellin Mackay's Bored Debutantes Are Satirized by Scott Fitzgerald[1]

Chicago Tribune European Edition / 1925

F. Scott Fitzgerald, young American novelist, author of *This Side of Paradise, Flappers and Philosophers,* and *The Great Gatsby,* and the popularly accredited delineator of the American girl, both in and out of society, yesterday took occasion to attack Miss Ellin Mackay in an interview with the *Tribune.* Mr. Fitzgerald is at present staying in Paris.

Miss Mackay is the well-known New York society girl, the daughter of Mr. Clarence H. Mackay, who in the current number of the *New Yorker* herself took occasion to attack the "hundreds of pale-faced youths," with whom the New York debutante has come to be forced to tolerate, and to extenuate the growing tendency of the modern girl to seek diversion in cabarets.[2]

Mr. Fitzgerald's remarks yesterday, made in somewhat satiric vein, are in the nature of a wrathy comeback at Miss Mackay, for in her article she wrote that "the trouble with our elders is that they have swallowed too much of F. Scott Fitzgerald . . . and believe all the backstairs gossip written about us."

"I have been reading recently about the great discovery of that celebrated intellectual, Miss Ellin Mackay," said Mr. Fitzgerald, "that sometimes society can be dull and that escape from it is to be found only in the cabaret. Miss Mackay evidently does not know that the debutante is not the only one who must escape from something. The innocent middle westerners at Yale and Princeton must also escape from the interminable engraved cards which they receive to inform them that their presence is requested at the debut of the Miss Ellin Mackays' ladies whom they have perhaps never had the honor of meeting.

"Personally I never accepted any such invitations, though I remember the

---

[1] Rewritten by Henry Wales as "N.Y. '400' Apes Chicago Manner; Fails; So Dull," *Chicago Daily Tribune,* 7 December 1925, p. 12.

[2] "Why We Go to Cabarets: A Post-Debutante Explains," *The New Yorker,* 1 (26 November 1925), pp. 7–8.

great debacle at the debut of Miss Kahn when one humorous reveller put in his pocket all the special Sherry's[3] silver and then fell on the parterre with a notable crash.

"The New York that Miss Mackay grew up in is a dull place. Its manners come from London or Chicago, or, frequently, from its own demimonde. What Miss Mackay wants to say, I think, is simply that life among those who are too stupid to buy the purchasable pepper of art is unbearably dull. People simply have to escape from a milieu largely composed of young women who write articles for the newspapers about the necessity of escaping from such a milieu."

Having thus disposed of Miss Mackay, the young novelist launched into a eulogy of Chicago as compared with New York. He remarked in passing that he knew the society of Chicago better than he did that of New York, and that his impressions of the latter were such as any casual visitor would be sure to get.

"Chicago," he said, "like London, has a personality, whereas the tone of New York society has always been imitative of the most conspicuously anemic side of English manners. What life it has had, has always come from Chicago.

"In passing, is it not true, as Mr. H. L. Mencken says, that the skyscraper is a Chicago product?

"But this is deviating from the main point, which is that the cheap snobbery exemplified once by such a person as Ward McAllister[4] is as typical of the inadequacy of American culture as the failure to produce any more substantial artistic form than the revue is typical of New York's lack of artistic vitality."

---

[3] Louis Sherry's restaurant in Manhattan.
[4] Nineteenth-century New Yorker who identified the five hundred people who constituted high society.

That Sad Young Man

John Chapin Mosher / 1926

Reprinted from the *New Yorker*, 2 (17 April 1926), pp. 20–21. Originally published in *The New Yorker*. Copyright © 1926 The New Yorker Magazine, Inc. Reprinted by permission. All rights reserved.

All was quiet on the Riviera, and then the Fitzgeralds arrived, Scott and Zelda and Scotty. The summer season opened. There had been talk about their coming. They were coming; they were not. One day they appeared on the beach. They had played tennis the day before, and were badly burned. Everybody was concerned about their burns. They must keep their shoulders covered; they must rub on olive oil. Scott was too burned to go in the water, and much of the time, he sat aside from the rush of things, a reflective, staid paterfamilias.

That the Fitzgeralds are the best looking couple in modern literary society doesn't do them justice, knowing what we do about beauty and brains. That they might be the handsomest pair at any collegiate houseparty, inspiring alumni to warnings about the pitfalls ahead of the young, is more to the point, although Scott really looks more as the undergraduate would like to look, than the way he generally does. It takes some years of training as the best host of the younger set, and as a much photographed and paragraphed author, to be quite so affable and perfectly at ease with all the world.

Scott feels that he is getting on in years, that he is no longer young. It weighs upon him, troubles him. He is almost thirty. Seldom has he allowed a person of such advanced age to enter his books.

"I have written a story. It is not about the younger generation. The hero is twenty-nine."

It must be some comfort to him that he is so superbly preserved, so stocky, muscular, clear-skinned, with wide, fresh, green-blue eyes, hair, blond not grey, with no lines of worry or senility, no saggings anywhere. Mrs. Fitzgerald doesn't show her age either; she might be in her 'teens. Perhaps Scotty does. Yes, there is no denying she looks her four.

There were rumors that Scott had had a sip or two of something up in Paris, and had come South to rest. No one could have guessed it, but he is summary with any such doubts:

"Don't you know I am one of the most notorious drinkers of the younger generation?"

There have been whispers certainly. But the young man who drives his publicity manager into a lake, as Scott once did, is bound to get some reputation of that sort.[1] There was no reason on this occasion why he should not have turned the car to the right as most people did, and as the publicity man comfortably expected, but having had perhaps a cocktail or two, it seemed more amusing to turn to the left off the road. The publicity man was not drowned however.

That was after one of those Long Island parties which established his place before the world as a host. If he is worried now about the advancing years he had better buy up two or three Biltmores before he extends that general invitation:

"Grow old along with me!

"The best is yet to be—."

This popularity on two continents may explain something of the financial mystery which so appals him. Ever since *This Side of Paradise*, money has poured in upon this young couple, thousands and thousands a month. And just as fast it has poured out. Where it goes, no one seems to know. Least of all evidently, the Fitzgeralds. They complain that nothing is left to show for it. Mrs. Fitzgerald hasn't even a pearl necklace.

According to Scott he has known poverty. There was the terrible winter after the war, when he wanted to marry Zelda, and had only a ninety-dollar-a-month advertising job and no prospects. He had gone South to see her, and when they parted at the station he hadn't even enough money for a Pullman. He had to climb into a Pullman, and then sneak through into the day coach.

It was then that he saw that advertising did not pay, and he threw up that job, and went home to St. Paul to write a novel. Statistics show that 12,536 young men annually throw up their jobs and go back home to write a novel. This has all come about since Fitzgerald set the example, for the book he wrote that winter was *This Side of Paradise*, and he was launched.

His success as an author was a great surprise to the home circle. He had always lived in St. Paul, but the Fitzgeralds were not what is known as literary people, in spite of their descent from the author of the "Star Spangled Banner." Scott's father was in business, and Scott was never addicted to prowling

---

[1] In the summer of 1923 Fitzgerald drove his editor Maxwell Perkins into a pond on Long Island.

about the public library. He was much too attractive a boy to be allowed much seclusion.

However he did enjoy scrawling notebooks full of various suggestions and impressions and witticisms, when the other faithful students of the St. Paul Academy and later those of the Newman School as well were busy adding and subtracting and wondering over what takes the ablative. In the Newman School he decided to run off a musical comedy, and two years later he spent his whole freshman year at Princeton writing the Triangle Show, which left him no time for algebra, trigonometry, coordinate geometry, and hygiene. But the Triangle Club accepted the show, and he tutored his way back to college and acted in his own work as a chorus girl.

The war came next, and as aide-de-camp to General J. F. Ryan he was able to spend his Saturday afternoons writing a hundred and twenty-thousand word novel, "The Romantic Egotist," which was merely a preparatory exercise apparently. Publishers thought it original and very well written, but not quite what they were looking for at the moment. A great many publishers were in that frame of mind about it,[2] but they did not manage to extinguish the writing impetus in him. The winter after the war, before he took up advertising, he collected 122 rejection slips, and by way of encouragement sold one story for $30.

Never has he lived that amorphous affair known as the literary life. He is too active for that, and too gregarious. To the younger set of St. Paul he was known as a dining-out, dancing-out country-club boy, and it was a surprise when it was said about that he wanted to write. But literary people there didn't take his ambitions as a joke. He became a great friend of Charles Flandrau's, who twenty years ago published *Harvard Episodes*, stories of freshmen and sophomores, done somewhat in the Henry James manner. There is no resemblance between the Flandrau book and Fitzgerald's, but with Mr. Flandrau, Scott found a sympathetic and intelligent critic, someone who could understand why he chose rather to write than to sell bonds. He had already begun to work with an energy unflagging in spite of his invitations to dinner. It sustained him even through the arduous business of rewriting *This Side of Paradise*, changing it, at his publisher's advice from the first to the third person.

Such application, of course, is not associated with the temperament of any

---

[2] The novel was not submitted to "a great many publishers." It may have been sent to another publisher after Scribners declined it, but there is no proof.

merely clever young man. The popular picture of a blond boy scribbling off bestsellers in odd moments between parties is nonsense. He's a very grave, hardworking man, and shows it. In fact there is definitely the touch of the melancholy often obvious upon him.

He is wary of the limitations of his experience.

Very deliberately he has taken as the field for his talent the great story of American wealth. His research is in the chronicles of the big business juntos of the last fifty years; and the drama of high finance, with the personalities of the major actors, Harriman, Morgan, Hill, is his serious study. He saw how the money was being spent; he has made it his business to ferret out how it was cornered.

Although Mrs. Fitzgerald once bought a bond, no young people, with such an income, are more far removed from the ordinary affairs of business. A twenty-dollar-a-week clerk must know more of the practical business world than Scott Fitzgerald who cannot live on thirty thousand a year, and yet who earns every cent he has.

His information, to be sure, on the general history of this American phase is remarkable. His most trivial stories have a substantial substratum of information.

It should yield more and more revealing, penetrating pictures of American life as he settles gravely down in the twilight of the thirties.

Where the French Outclass Us
Unlocated / 1926

Probably in a New York newspaper, December 1926. Reprinted from
Fitzgerald's scrapbook.

Scott Fitzgerald, the novelist, has just returned from a sojourn abroad. He
celebrated his arrival with some provocative observations. They concerned
Americans and other peoples, and in some respects were not so complimen-
tary to his home folks. The French—the novelist reluctantly conceded—are
as far above us as we are above the African in an understanding of life.
Americans are a race of children, forever in pursuit of some new toy; always
looking forward, never enjoying the moment; and, consequently, the most
unhappy people in the world.

Fitzgerald may be right about it, but his observations are well calculated
to start debate. All depends upon the definition of happiness. Life for Americans from the beginning has been a pursuit, a looking forward; and it may
be, because the urge is inherent and ineradicable, that in some field of activity
lies their only hope of happiness. The American's happiness is linked with
progress.

The novelist should have extended his remarks so that we may know in
what ways the French have attained to a better understanding of life than we
have. Perhaps it is his private intention to do that in a later book. But a doubt
of the accuracy of his observation will persist until he dispels it.

Scott Fitzgerald Lays Success to Reading[1]

Gilmore Millen / 1927

Los Angeles Evening Herald, 15 January 1927, pp. A2, A4. Reprinted
by permission of the *Los Angeles Times*.

F. Scott Fitzgerald, who left Princeton when he was twenty-one and wrote a
book that made every critic in the country hail him as the interpreter of the
youth of the Jazz Age—

Who has written dozens of stories about flappers and gin parties and wild
dizzy nights maddened by muted saxophones—

Who, at the age of thirty, is certainly the youngest, and possibly the most
brilliant, of the younger generation of American authors—

Acquired the literary ability which provided him with a luxurious room
overlooking the vivid green lawns of the Ambassador Hotel, in a very ordinary, but serious manner.

He did it by reading books—the best books.

He smoked cigarets from a fifteen-cent package, rumpled his close cut
blonde hair, fixed a tie that tried to spring away from its moorings around a
soft collar beneath a well-tailored olive gray sack suit, and told all about it
today, smiling unconsciously and pleasantly, as though nothing unusual had
ever happened in his life after all.

He had been talking about Europe—the Riviera and the Bay of Naples and
Paris—where he has been living, with his charming wife, who came from
Montgomery, Ala., for the past three years.

There was the literary crowd in Paris—the American literary crowd—to
be described. He had to mention James Joyce, who wrote *Ulysses*, and Gertrude Stein, who wrote *Three Lives* and started half the present school of
American writers on their way of writing and finally, Ernest Hemingway,
former sparring partner for Sam Langford, ex-newspaperman and American
war hero on the Italian front.

Then he was persuaded to talk about himself—about his intellectual devel-

---

[1] This interview was substantially repeated in Muriel Babcock, "F. Scott Fitzgerald
Upholds His Own Generation," an unlocated clipping in Fitzgerald's scrapbook.

opment, about the books he had read; about the books that he thought were the best books ever written. He was asked to name his list of "10 best books." But he wouldn't. He said:

"I'm thirty now. I've been reading since I was fourteen—that is, books have been influencing me since I was fourteen. So I will try to name, one for each two years during the past sixteen years, the books I have read that have been the greatest influence on my mind."

He found a pencil (he always uses a pencil instead of a typewriter when he writes) and wrote down, after much crossing out and revising, the following table:

At 14, *The Varmint*—Owen Johnson
At 16, *The Lord of the World*—Robert Hugh Benson
At 18, *The Picture of Dorian Gray*—Oscar Wilde
At 20, *Sinister Street*—Compton Mackenzie
At 22, *Tony Bungay*—H. G. Wells[2]
At 24, *The Genealogy of Morals*—Friedrich Neitzsche
At 26, *The Brothers Karamazov*—Fyodor Dostoievski
At 28, *Ludendorff's Memoirs*
At 30, *The Decline of the West*—Oswald Spengler

He talked about American literature. He thought that Theodore Dreiser is the greatest living American author.

"*An American Tragedy*," he said, "is without doubt the greatest American book that has appeared in years."

But, being a young writer, he is most concerned and interested in the work of other young writers, chiefly John Dos Passos, Ernest Hemingway, and e. e. cummings.

Then Mrs. Fitzgerald came into the room. She is blonde, with bobbed hair, and you remember, southern—from Montgomery, Ala. She has a southern drawl that makes you think of white houses with tall columns on the front porch, and of hot black fields where the negroes sang blues songs that were first hummed on the Congo, and of bob whites calling in the spring time, when the rows of young cotton plants stretch out like long green ribbons.

She knows a great deal about books, too. She sat down, talked for a few minutes, compared the style of a certain much lauded young woman writer to the twisted, inverted style of the late Henry James, and went out again.

---

[2] Wells's 1908 novel was titled *Tono-Bungay*.

And the author of *The Great Gatsby* lit another cigaret from his fifteen-cent package for himself and one for a newspaperman, and went on talking. He didn't have anything to say about the present day flappers in America, because he hadn't seen many lately. He and Mrs. Fitzgerald have been in Europe for the past three years. They got back three weeks ago, visited the old home of Mrs. Fitzgerald in Montgomery, Ala., and then came west, to Los Angeles.

"I was shocked when I returned to America," he said. "I had been, you know, three years in Paris. I saw shows on the New York stage which would have shocked the French.

"Everything in New York seems mouldy, rotten. We went to the night clubs. It was like going to a big mining camp in the boom days.

"In Texas Guinan's[3] I got a sensation of horror. There were these fat men smoking fat cigars, and big butter and egg men, and half nude women. There was nothing fine about it all. It was vulgarity without the faintest trace of redeeming wit.

"Coming from Paris to New York was like plunging from a moral world to a state of moral anarchy.

"It gave me a fear that everyone had gone crazy—that everything was being done for nothing; that human lives were being exploited for nothing.

"And it's not the fault of prohibition. Prohibition is just a crazy symptom of a crazy race. I don't know what it is. Perhaps America just came too late—too late to be anything in our own right, but just part of the history and tradition of Europe.

"The country seems like warmed over hash—warmed over from the day before. America is the place where everybody is always going to have a good time tomorrow.

"There is nothing, no tradition, no background, that you can summon when you say you are an American, as you can if you could say you were an Englishman, or even a Frenchman.

"It perhaps was different, in the days of Washington and Hamilton and Tom Payne—but it is not so now!"

But almost immediately after these gloomy observations, Mr. Fitzgerald became cheerful. The subject of his new novel was mentioned. He really can't help being cheerful and pleasant, it seems, despite the fact that he has just finished reading *The Decline of the West*, and the further fact that he named a book by Nietzsche among the books that had influenced him most.

---

[3] Manhattan speakeasy.

He was all excited about his new novel, which won't appear for some months yet.[4] He thinks it is the best thing that he has done.

"I keep myself pure in regard to my novels," he said, seriously. "I have written only three of them. Each one takes two or three years. Of course, there are my short stories—but, then, you have to live—"

And he was going to read the first three pages of that novel. But it was getting late. And he had been so very affable and good natured and pleasant, talking two hours about a hundred and one matters, literary gossip, stories of the great he has met and so on—

That, it was really time to end what was more of a conversation than an interview.

And then, too, Mrs. Fitzgerald was coming back from across the hall, in Carmel Meyers's[5] room, where she went to get the telephone number of a dressmaker.

So he said, "Good Bye"—this affable young Princetonian, who writes about jazz and flappers, and reads and thinks more seriously than most older writers, who write about what they think are weightier subjects.

---

[4] Fitzgerald's fourth novel was not published until 1934.
[5] Movie star whom the Fitzgeralds had first met in Rome in 1925.

Fitzgerald, Spenglerian

Harry Salpeter / 1927

F. Scott Fitzgerald is a Nietzschean, F. Scott Fitzgerald is a Spenglerian,[1] F. Scott Fitzgerald is in a state of cosmic despair. From within his slightly shuttered eyes, F. Scott Fitzgerald looks out upon a world which is doomed, in his sight, to destruction; from his unbearded lips comes conviction of America that is as final as the sentence is harsh. Summation of the evidence and conviction came in such a rush of words, in such a tumbling of phrase upon phrase that neither objection nor appeal was possible. It was a rush of words which only powerful feeling could dictate. Here was I interviewing the author of *This Side of Paradise,* the voice and embodiment of the jazz age, its product and its beneficiary, a popular novelist, a movie scenarist, a dweller in the gilded palaces, a master of servants, only to find F. Scott Fitzgerald, himself, shorn of these associations, forecasting doom, death, and damnation to his generation, in the spirit, if not in the rhetoric, of your typical spittoon philosopher. In a pleasant corner of the Plaza[2] tea garden he sounded like an intellectual Samson prophesying the crumbling of its marble columns. He looks like a candid, serious youth. His blue eyes, fair hair and clean-cut profile, no less than his reputation, give the lie to the mind of F. Scott Fitzgerald.

I had caught Fitzgerald at the Plaza, his midway stop between Hollywood where, after much travail, he had completed a scenario for Constance Talmadge,[3] and Brandywine Hundred, Del.,[4] an address which tickles him. There he will make his home for the next two years and there he will complete his next novel. This, he said, had been vaguely suggested by the Loeb-Leopold[5]

---

[1] References to German philosophers Friedrich Nietzsche (1844–1900) and Oswald Spengler (1880–1936). Nietzsche attacked the "slave morality" of Christianity, and Spengler believed that Western civilization was in decline.

[2] The Plaza Hotel in New York.

[3] Fitzgerald's screenplay for actress Talmadge was rejected.

[4] "Ellerslie," the mansion Fitzgerald was renting, was near Wilmington, Delaware.

[5] Chicagoans Richard Loeb and Nathan Leopold committed an "intellectual murder" in 1924. The early version of the novel that became *Tender Is the Night* had the working title "The Boy Who Killed His Mother."

case and in the tragic moments of this novel will be mirrored some of the cosmic despair under the burden of which Fitzgerald manages, somehow, to maintain a resilient step.

And after this novel—on which he has already worked three years—is completed?

Why, what is there left to do? Go to pieces. Or write another novel. A writer is good only for writing and showing off. Then people find him out or he runs out of money and then he goes and writes another novel.

Fitzgerald has been "a hot Nietzschean" ever since he read *Thus Spake Zarathustra.*[6] Today, Oswald Spengler's *Decline of the West*[7] is his "bedbook." What have Nietzsche and Spengler in common? "Spengler stands on the shoulders of Nietzsche and Nietzsche on those of Goethe." This civilization has nothing more to produce. "We threw up our fine types in the eighteenth century, when we had Beethoven and Goethe. The race had a mind then." All that there is left to do is to go into a period of universal hibernation and begin all over again at the sheep-grazing stage. He said:

Spenglerism signals the death of this civilization. We are in a period paralleling Rome 185 years after Christ, Greece just before Alexander, the Mohammedan world about 1200. There is now no mind of the race, there is now no great old man of the tribe, there are no longer any feet to sit at. People have to stage sham battles in their own minds.

Mussolini, the last slap in the face of liberalism, is an omen for America. America is ready for an Alexander, a Trajan, or a Constantine. The idea that we're the greatest people in the world because we have the most money in the world is ridiculous. Wait until this wave of prosperity is over! Wait ten or fifteen years! Wait until the next war on the Pacific, or against some European combination! Then we shall have to fight for our race and not under the leadership of a Calvin Coolidge.

The next fifteen years will show how much resistance there is in the American race. The only thing that can make it worth while to be an American is a life and death struggle, a national testing. After that it may be possible for a man to say 'I'm an American' as a man might say 'I'm a Frenchman' or 'I'm a German,' or, until recently, when the colonies made cowards of them all, 'I'm an Englishman.' The good American is the best in the world, as an individual. But taken collectively, he is a mass product without common sense or guts or dignity.

---

[6] Published in four parts between 1883 and 1892.

[7] First published in English translation 1926–1928. Fitzgerald did not read German.

At present writing, this descendant of the author of "The Star-Spangled Banner" is not proud to be an American. "I have never said I was an American." That descendant can say: "Better that an entire Division should have been wiped out than that Otto Braun should have been killed." Braun, a German boy, at the age of nineteen or twenty, gave such evidences of genius that he was regarded as a Goethe in the budding. He was killed in the Argonne during the advance of the 77th Division.

Yet the man who is not proud to be an American is an American, if descent, on one side, from landholders on grant who came in 1630 means anything. On one side, said Fitzgerald, he comes from straight 1850 potato-famine Irish who prospered with the rising Middle West; and, on the other, from sometimes prosperous, sometimes indigent, but always proud, Maryland stock, who threw off, among other freaks, Philip Key, the manufacturer who made, without charge, all the buttons on the Continental uniforms, and Francis Scott Key.

We talked about the American in Paris, to which city Fitzgerald sometimes goes in quest of refuge from America.

The best of America drifts to Paris. The American in Paris is the best American. It is more fun for an intelligent person to live in an intelligent country. France has the only two things toward which we drift as we grow older—intelligence and good manners.

And why isn't it any fun to be an American?

Because it's too big to get your hands on. Because it's a woman's country. Because its very nice and its various local necessities have made it impossible for an American to have a real credo. After all, an American is condemned to saying "I don't like this." He has never had time—and I mean time, the kind of inspired hush that people make for themselves in which to want to be or to do on the scale and with all the arrogant assumptions with which great races make great dreams. There has never been an American tragedy. There have only been great failures. That is why the story of Aaron Burr—let alone that of Jefferson Davis—opens up things that we who accept the United States as an established unit hardly dare to think about.

Fitzgerald is distrait. He can't call himself a liberal. Finding liberalism "mushy and ineffectual," he is compelled to turn to the Mussolini-Ludendorff idea. He does and does not want Mussolini. "If you're against Mussolini you're for the cesspool that Italy was before him. If you're for Mussolini you're for Caesarism." To call one's self a Communist is no solution either. Fitzgerald's hope for the nation lies in the birth of a hero who will be of age when America's testing comes. It is possible that an American woman may be big enough of soul to bear and nurture such a hero; it is more likely that he will come out of the immigrant class, in the guise of an eastside newsboy. "His mother will be a good woman, in the sense that Otto Braun's mother was; she knew that he was a hero. But when this American hero is born one knows that he will not be brought up by the reading of liberal magazines, nor educated by women teachers." The father, said Fitzgerald, doesn't matter. Behind Fitzgerald's pessimism there is mysticism.

Has the Flapper Changed?

Margaret Reid / 1927

Reprinted from *Motion Picture Magazine,* 33 (July 1927), pp. 28–29, 104. Copyright © *Motion Picture Magazine,* a Macfadden-Bartell publication. Reprinted by permission.

The term "flapper" has become a generalization, meaning almost any *femme* between fifteen and twenty-five. Some five years ago it was a thing of distinction—indicating a neat bit of femininity, collegiate age, who rolled her stockings, chain-smoked, had a heavy "line," mixed and drank a mean highball and radiated "It."

The manner in which the title has come into such general usage is a little involved, but quite simple. A young man wrote a book. His heroine was one of the n. bits of f. referred to above. "Flapper" was her official classification. The man's book took the country by, as they say, storm. Girls—all girls—read it. They read about the flapper's deportment, methods, and career. And with a nice simultaneousness they became, as nearly as their varied capabilities permitted, flappers. Thus the frequency of the term today. I hope you get my point.

The young man responsible for it all, after making clear—in his book—the folly of flappers' ways, married the young person who had been the prototype for the character and started in to enjoy the royalties. The young man was F. Scott Fitzgerald, the book was *This Side of Paradise*, and the flapper's name was Zelda. So about six years later they came to Hollywood and Mr. Fitzgerald wrote a screen story for Constance Talmadge. Only people don't call him Mr. Fitzgerald. They call him "Scotty."

But we don't seem to be getting anywhere. The purpose of this discursion was to hear Mr. F. Scott (or Scotch) Fitzgerald's opinion of the cinema descendants of his original brain-daughter, the Flapper.

It was with an admirable attempt to realize the seriousness of my mission that I went to his bungalow at the Ambassador. Consider, tho! By all literary standards he should have been a middle-aged gentleman with too much waistline, too little hair and steel-rimmed spectacles. And I knew, from pictures in *Vanity Fair* and hysterical firsthand reports, that instead he was probably the best-looking thing ever turned out of Princeton. Or even (in crescendo) Harvard—or Yale. Only it was Princeton. Add "It," and the charming, vibrant, brilliant mind his work projects. My interest was perhaps a bit more than professional.

There was a large tray on the floor at the door of his suite when I reached it. On the tray were bottles of Canada Dry, some oranges, a bowl of cracked ice and—three very, very empty Bourbon bottles. There was also a card. I paused before ringing the bell and bent down to read the inscription—"With Mr. Van Vechten's kindest regards to Scott and Zelda Fitzgerald." I looked for any further message on the other side, but there was none, so I rang the bell.

It was answered by a young man of medium height. With Prince-of-Wales hair and eyes that are, I am sure, green. His features are chiseled finely. His mouth draws your attention. It is sensitive, taut and faintly contemptuous, and even in the flashing smile does not lose the indication of intense pride.

Behind him was Mrs. Fitzgerald, the *Rosamund* of *This Side of Paradise.* Slim, pretty like a rather young boy; with one of those schoolgirl complexions and clear gray eyes; her hair as short as possible, slicked back. And dressed as only New Yorkers intangibly radiate smartness.

The two of them might have stepped, sophisticated and charming, from the pages of any of the Fitzgerald books.

They greeted me and discovered the tray hilariously.

"Carl Van Vechten's going-away gift," the First Flapper of the Land explained in her indolent, Alabama drawl. "He left this morning after a week's stay. Said he came here for a little peace and rest, and he disrupted the entire colony."

In the big, dimly lit room, Mrs. Fitzgerald sank sighing into a chair. She had just come from a Black Bottom[1] lesson. F. Scott moved restlessly from chair to chair. He had just come from a studio conference and I think he'd rather have been at the Horse Show. He was also a trifle disconcerted by the impending interview. In one he had given to an avid press lady the day before, he had said all his bright remarks. And he couldn't think up any more in such a short time.

"What, tho, were his opinions of screen flappers? As flappers? As compared to his Original Flappers?"

"Well, I can only," he began, lighting a cigaret, putting it out and crossing

---

[1] Dance similar to the Charleston, it was inspired by the DaSylva-Henderson-Brown song "Black Bottom."

to another chair, "speak about the immediate present. I know nothing of their evolution. You see, we've been living on the Riviera for three years. In that time the only movies we've seen have been a few of the very old pictures, or the Westerns they show over there. I might," his face brightening, "tell you what I think of Tom Mix."

"Scotty!" his wife cautioned quickly.

"Oh, well. . . ."

Having exhausted all the available chairs in the room, he returned to the first one and began all over again.

"Have flappers changed since you first gave them the light of publicity? For better? For worse?"

"Only in the superficial matter of clothes, haircut, and wisecracks. Fundamentally they are the same. The girls I wrote about were not a type—they were a generation. Free spirits—evolved thru the war chaos and a final inevitable escape from restraint and inhibitions. If there is a difference, it is that the flappers today are perhaps less defiant, since their freedom is taken for granted and they are sure of it. In my day—stroking his hoary beard—they had just made their escape from dull and blind conventionality. Subconsciously there was a hint of belligerence in their attitude, because of the opposition they met—but overcame.

"On the screen, of course, is represented every phase of flapper life. But just as the screen exaggerates action, so it exaggerates type. The girl who, in real life, uses a smart, wisecracking line is portrayed on the screen as a hard-boiled baby. The type, one of the most dangerous, whose forte is naiveté, approximates a dumb-dora when she reaches the screen. The exotic girl becomes bizarre. But the actresses who do flappers really well understand them thoroughly enough to accentuate their characteristics without distorting them."

"How about Clara Bow?" I suggested, starting in practically alphabetical order.

"Clara Bow is the quintessence of what the term 'flapper' signifies as a definite description. Pretty, impudent, superbly assured, as worldly wise, briefly clad and 'hard-berled' as possible. There were hundreds of them—her prototypes. Now, completing the circle, there are thousands more—patterning themselves after her.

"Colleen Moore represents the young collegiate—the carefree, lovable child who rules bewildered but adoring parents with an iron hand. Who beats her brothers and beaus on the tennis courts, dances like a professional and has infallible methods for getting her own way. All deliciously celluloid—but why not? The public notoriously prefer glamor to realism. Pictures like Miss Moore's flapper epics present a glamorous dream of youth and gaiety and swift, tapping feet. Youth—actual youth—is essentially crude. But the movies idealize it, even as Gershwin idealizes jazz in the Rhapsody in Blue.

"Constance Talmadge is the epitome of young sophistication. She is the deft princess of lingerie—and love—plus humor. She is Fifth Avenue and diamonds and Catalya orchids and Europe every year. She is sparkling and witty and as gracefully familiar with the new books as with the new dances. I have an idea that Connie appeals every bit as strongly to the girls in the audience as to the men. Her dash—her zest for things—is compelling. She is the flapper *de luxe*.

"I happened to see a preview the other night, at a neighborhood movie house near here. It was Milton Sills's latest, I am told. There was a little girl in it—playing a tough baby-vamp. I found that her name was Alice White. She was a fine example of the European influence on our flappers. Gradually, due mostly to imported pictures, the vogue for 'pose' is fading.

"European actresses were the first to disregard personal appearance in emotional episodes. Disarranged hair—the wrong profile to the camera— were of no account during a scene. Their abandonment to emotion precluded all thought of beauty. Pola Negri brought it to this country. It was adopted by some. But the flappers seem to have been a bit nervous as to the results. It was, perhaps, safer to be cute than character. This little White girl, however, appears to have a flair for this total lack of studied effect. She is the flapper impulsive—child of the moment—wildly eager for every drop of life. She represents—not the American flapper—but the European.

"Joan Crawford is doubtless the best example of the dramatic flapper. The girl you see at the smartest night clubs—gowned to the apex of sophistication—toying iced glasses, with a remote, faintly bitter expression—dancing deliciously—laughing a great deal with wide, hurt eyes. It takes girls of actual talent to get away with this in real life. When they do perfect the thing, they have a lot of fun with it.

"Then, inevitably, there is the quality that is infallible in any era, any town, any time. Femininity, *ne plus ultra*. Unless it is a very definite part of a girl, it is insignificant, and she might as well take up exoticism. But sufficiently apparent, it is always irresistible. I suppose she isn't technically a flapper—but because she *is* Femininity, one really should cite Vilma Banky. Soft and gentle and gracious and sweet—all the lacy adjectives apply to her.

This type is reticent and unassuming—but just notice the quality of orchids on her shoulder as she precedes her reverential escort into the theater.

"It's rather futile to analyze flappers. They are just girls—all sorts of girls. Their one common trait being that they are young things with a splendid talent for life."

F. Scott Fitzgerald

Charles G. Shaw / 1928

Reprinted from *The Low-Down* (New York: Henry Holt, 1928), pp. 163–69. Copyright © Charles G. Shaw. Reprinted by permission of Holt, Rinehart & Winston.

F. Scott Fitzgerald, the son of Edward and Mary Fitzgerald, was born in St. Paul, Minnesota, on the twenty-fourth of September, 1896. He is a mixture of Irish and Maryland English. Francis Scott Key Fitzgerald is his full name, Francis Scott Key having been a brother of his great-grandfather.

The Newman School of Hackensack, N.J., and, later Princeton University (which he left in 1917 to join the army) served as his educational fields, though in point of fact he is actually self-educated.

He is essentially romantic, egoistic and somewhat vain.

This Side of Paradise was his first novel, published in 1920, the year of his marriage to Zelda Sayre of Montgomery, Alabama.

Among his favored gastronomic interests are *petite marmite,* sole *meuniere,* duck with orange sauce, mushroom soup, and partridge with currant jelly. He looks with small favor, however, upon bird's nest pudding or Algerian *kous-kous.*

As a youth, he yearned to be a famous football star and "king of the world" (neither of which desires has left him since). He is congenitally shy but the fact is efficiently concealed.

His early habits of reckless extravagance were an outgrowth of trying to keep up with others whose incomes were many times his own.

He has written one play, *The Vegetable*—a comedy.

His suits, in hue, are usually of green or mauve and are made by Davies & Son, of 19–20 Hanover Street, London, W. I., while his shirts come from the shop of Hilditch & Key, also of London. His ties and pocket handkerchiefs are all brightly-colored.

He ordinarily rises about eleven o'clock and does most of his work from 5 P.M. to 3:30 A.M. He is left-handed in everything save writing. He will frequently talk to himself.

Belts refuse to hold up his trousers.

He believes that happiness consists of the performances of all the natural functions, with one exception—that of growing old. Sunday, Washington, D.C., cold weather, Bohemians, the managing type of American woman, avarice, and dullness are his principal dislikes.

From childhood he had intended to be a writer and entered Princeton with the plan of writing the Triangle Club musical comedies.

He is a member of the Cottage Club of Princeton.

His best-loved beverages are Pouilly, Mersault, Arbois, and Pilsner, and his favorite literary piece—Spengler's *Decline of the West*.

Chaplin's *The Pilgrim* is his pet motion-picture, and *The Playboy of the Western World* his favorite play.

He has almost always lived in the country and made spasmodic excursions into town, the French Riviera and New York City being his idea of the world's most frolicsome resorts.

When away from home, he usually carries a package of bromides.

The chief early influences on his life he believes to have been the Roman Catholic Church, John Peale Bishop's friendly tutelage in English poetry, the wealthy middle-west, his marriage, the works of Compton Mackenzie, Samuel Butler, H. G. Wells, and H. L. Mencken, together with certain friendships.

During the war he served as (1): first lieutenant of infantry and (2): aide-de-camp to Brigadier General J. A. Ryan in various training camps.

He dances only under pressure, and prefers, at a party, to talk or listen to the chatter of others. While drinking, he is able to stand almost any company, but prefers that of Celts, and when on gaiety bent, will never set out with any liquor on his person but ultimately purchase a bottle at some dubious drugstore, which he will convince himself is prewar stock.

He has always relished planning a trip or embarking upon a new piece of work.

He has spent three years in France and Italy and possesses a remarkable (and bloodcurdling) collection of stereoptical slides of the war, amassed while in Europe.[1] He would hate to live the rest of his life in Italy.

Currently, his favorite author is André Gide.

When writing, he is usually nervous and irritable and will engulf, during his labors, innumerable cups of Coca-Cola. He writes entirely in pencil and makes from two to four drafts, depending upon the class of work involved. While so engaged, he will consume about half a carton of Chesterfield cigarettes.

---

[1] Fitzgerald's glass slides are now in the Matthew J. and Arlyn Bruccoli Collection of F. Scott Fitzgerald, Thomas Cooper Library, University of South Carolina.

He will contract a hangover from work as well as from play.

For popular music he hands the first prize to Vincent Youmans.

Foyot's and La Reine Pedauque are his best-liked Parisian haunts, while in Rome he favors the Castello dei Cesari. In Cannes it is the *Café des Alliés*[2] and in New York the Meadowbrook and Caesar's.

His preference in women is a not-too-light blonde, who is intelligent, un-opinionated, and responsive.

He likes watching college football games and, for diversion, reading detective stories. Swimming is his chief outdoor exercise.

He is able to speak a rather bad French.

Scandal touching upon his friends, everything about the late war, discovering new men and books of promise, Princeton, and people with extraordinary personal charm are his greatest interests in life.

He parts his hair in the middle and his eyes are light green.

After a certain number of highballs, in some curious fashion, he will appear to have shrunk to about two-thirds of his ordinary size.

He is always ready to laugh at himself.

On an evening's outing, he has, time and again, purchased a newsboy's complete supply of morning papers, and tipped taxi drivers to the extent of paying the fare several times over.

He is able to put away, in a single session, a lay-out of gins, wines, whiskies, and liqueurs.

His headquarters in New York is the Plaza.

As to politics, he is an autocrat in theory but a socialist in practice, and with respect to the Younger Generation, he says, he feels like an old man.

Though by nature not at all Rabelaisian, he enjoys acting so when with people who are easily shocked.

---

[2] Café des Alleés.

Delaware-Paris: F. Scott Fitzgerald

Nino Frank / 1928

From an unidentified French newspaper. Reprinted from Fitzgerald's scrapbook. Translated by Philip Stewart.

Mr. Scott Fitzgerald cannot complain about his career as a man of letters: at twenty-two, on graduation from Princeton, he published his first book, *This Side of Paradise*, a satirical study of several flappers, liberated American girls, and two hundred thousand copies of the novel were sold with no problem. He has since published two other novels, one of which is *The Great Gatsby* which Mr. Victor Llona has superbly translated,[1] and three volumes of stories, greeted by the same success. At thirty-one, the thin, blond boy with piercing eyes and a childish laugh is one of the authors most in vogue across the Atlantic: he notes this but is unmoved by it, and confesses that he prefers his months of vacation in France to his mansion in Delaware.

"The influence of French writers in America is very great: first of all Proust, whose complete work is in the process of being translated. *Sodome et Gomorrhe* has just been issued in a private edition, out of fear of the public. This does not keep writers like Hemingway, cummings, and especially Thornton Wilder, author of *The Bridge of San Luis Rey*, who is coming to Europe with his friend Gene Tunney, from being the most original among the most original among the young writers, and thoroughly accepting Proust's importance. Gide, who had a big success with *Les Caves du Vatican*[2] seems to us diminished since the publication of *Les Faux-monnayeurs*[3]; he has now been captured by the snobs, who on the other hand will not touch Proust. For my part, while I recognize the greatness of the French mind, I confess I owe what I know to English writers; maybe I should add English writers who spoke French. Joyce, Compton Mackenzie—these are my masters. . . . Dreiser, Lewis, and especially Anderson, are the most prominent men on the American literary front today: we all owe something to Anderson. . . . Our avant-garde writers are uninteresting; the likes of Hemingway or Wilder are much more daring. You see, we really cannot be interested in the mechanical

---

[1] *Gatsby le magnifique.* Paris: Collection Européene, Kra Edit, 1926.

[2] *Lafcadio's Adventures.*

[3] *The Counterfeiters.*

life, in everything that has enchanted European poets: for us that is nothing extraordinary; we are looking for other themes, closer to our dreams. . . . Certainly American life today easily lends itself to satire: women absolutely dominate. They are organized against the men, whose intelligence, it seems to me, moreover, is becoming feminine. We do not react: and I would be delighted if this were to be the dawn of a new civilization of Amazons, but alas! . . . In exchange, the men have become more dishonest. As for the Negroes. . . . Better not talk about that; it's too complicated. Life is really strange in America. I much prefer France: here, I am comfortable; here everything is seen from a more genuine, cordial point of view. I am working hard and well: but I dare not yet write anything about France. . . ."

Fitzgerald Finds He Has Outgrown Jazz Novel Age

Unlocated / 1929

Possibly in the *Chicago Tribune European Edition,* ca. Fall 1929. Reprinted from Fitzgerald's scrapbook.

Mr. F. Scott Fitzgerald feels that he is "dated." Although only thirty-three years old, this American writer, who is finishing a novel in Paris—his first since 1925—is mindful that he has left far behind him the type of youth and girl, the fast, irrepressible, drinking and necking young people, of his early books.

"When I see a girl of eighteen I realize that the gap between her age and mine is enormous," Mr. Fitzgerald confessed yesterday in his home in the Etoile section. "My reactions are apt to be ridiculous. I am tempted to be the jolly old boy, with the accomplishments of ten years ago, the castle walk[1] or outmoded stories.

"Then there is a reaction. I become extremely grave and am likely to launch into serious preaching. But soon the remarks sound silly and if I am sensible, I give up, for I am dated: I belong to a certain age. Unless you are something in the marriage market, extravagantly wealthy, for instance, you are out of it so far as possessing much reality goes and assume for the young one about the same importance that her father would have—in giving the same preachment—and that is a vague importance indeed.

"Before thirty a man is 'contemporary,' but after that it's an unfortunate state of affairs when he is asked to give his opinion on the younger generation, an ever-fluctuating thing."

---

[1] Dance step introduced by Vernon and Irene Castle.

Scott Fitzgeralds to Spend Winter Here Writing Books

Walling Keith / 1931

Reprinted from the *Montgomery Advertiser,* 8 October 1931, pp. 1, 7.
Copyright © *Montgomery Advertiser.* Reprinted by permission.

F. Scott Fitzgerald, fiction writer and author of several novels, and Mrs. Fitzgerald, the former Miss Zelda Sayre, arrived in Montgomery yesterday to spend the winter. Their ten-year-old daughter, Scottie, will arrive Saturday.

Mrs. Fitzgerald, who is also a writer, is working on a book. They returned recently to New York from Europe where they had spent two years, gathering color for their writings.

At the Greystone Hotel where the Fitzgeralds are stopping until their home they have leased for the winter on Felder Avenue is fitted, Mr. Fitzgerald expressed delight in finding that Montgomery "showed less of signs of depression" than any American city that he has recently visited.

"The people here don't seem to recognize the existence of a depression," he declared, telling of his amazement at finding poor business conditions the chief topic of conversation everywhere he went after his return from Europe.

"In the East, even at places where people seek recreation and at parties where one goes to forget the day's work, it seemed that I hardly became acquainted with members of the party before they were talking of the depression. I'm going to like it here in Montgomery, I know. It's a relief to spend a few hours in a city where I'm not met with talk of depression."

In a conversation in which he discussed prohibition, national politics, current literature and writers, Communism and baseball, Mr. Fitzgerald touched upon the South and its typical cities.

"You see, I'm not a stranger to Montgomery at all," he explained. "Having been stationed here during the war and marrying a Montgomery girl, I have felt the warmness of the city's hospitality."

Mr. Fitzgerald, who said he was a Jeffersonian Democrat at heart and somewhat of a Communist in ideals, declared that the prohibition law was not only a foolish gesture but that it was a hindrance to the machine of government.

"Understand now, I'm purely a fiction writer and do not profess to be an earnest student of political science," he smiled, "but I believe strongly that such a law as one prohibiting liquor is foolish, and all the writers, keenly interested in human welfare whom I know, laugh at the prohibition law.

"Not only is the question a laughable one," he said, "but it has done more to prevent perfect coordination among the members of both major political parties than any one thing.

"This is not new. All of my writer friends think and say the same thing," he added hastily.

"Another great difference I have found since my few hours in Montgomery," he said, "is the seemingly lack of fear of communistic activity or thought here. It seems foolish for an American to be afraid of any communistic revolution in this country, right now, but I heard so many conjectures of possible reactions here, while in Eastern cities, that at times I felt myself becoming concerned with the question.

"In ideals, I am somewhat of a communist. That is, as much as other persons who belong to what we call 'the arts group'; but communism as I see it has no place in the United States," he laughed, "and the American people will not stand for its teachings."

Mr. Fitzgerald, who counts among his friends, many writers of national and international note, expressed a fondness for Alabama and showed interest in Southern writers.

Ernest Hemingway, whom he saw in New York several days ago, is finishing a new novel, Mr. Fitzgerald said. Ring Lardner, the humorist, a friend of Fitzgerald's whom he visited before coming to Montgomery, is seriously ill.

The novel on which Mr. Fitzgerald is now working will be his first one in four years. He is a regular contributor of short stories to the *Saturday Evening Post* and other magazines.

His novel *This Side of Paradise*, was published before his graduation from Princeton.[1]

"Since then I've been a professional writer, and I think I've been lucky," he said.

---

[1] Untrue. *This Side of Paradise* was published in 1920.

Scott Fitzgerald Seeking Home Here
Baltimore Sun / 1932

Reprinted from the *Baltimore Sun,* 8 May 1932, pp. 18, 12. Copyright © *Baltimore Sun.* Reprinted by permission.[1]

F. Scott Fitzgerald, of *This Side of Paradise* fame, let it be known here last night that the Fitzgeralds are about to become a two-novelist family.

From the bed she has occupied in the Johns Hopkins Hospital for the last six weeks, Mrs. Fitzgerald, who was Miss Zelda Sayre, of Montgomery, Ala., has sent her first novel to a publisher, he said.

The completion of Mrs. Fitzgerald's first novel—autobiographical at her husband's suggestion—was not the only news Mr. Fitzgerald had to impart. He said he had been looking about for a place so that he and Mrs. Fitzgerald and their ten-year-old daughter, Frances, might make their permanent home in the vicinity of Baltimore.

Mr. Fitzgerald, whose name has not appeared upon a new book since his *All the Sad Young Men* was published in 1926, was almost as happy about his wife's novel as he was about the fact that physicians have told him she should be able to leave the hospital in two weeks.

Mrs. Fitzgerald has been a semi-invalid for the last two years.

"She was training for the Russian ballet, but she had started too late; the strain was too hard for her," Mr. Fitzgerald said. "Then, Diaghilev died, and shortly after that Mrs. Fitzgerald had a complete nervous breakdown."

Her illness halted Mr. Fitzgerald's work on a new novel which had engaged him for two years. Now that she is recovering, he has returned to the novel, whose first chapter is four years old. He would divulge nothing of its nature, however.

"I hate to talk about an unfinished novel," he said. "These things change so while you're working on them."

While the novel has been gathering dust he has been busy writing short stories, approximately fifty having come from his pen. One, soon to be published, is called "Family in the Wind" and is based on his experiences in the tornadoes that recently swept part of Alabama.

---

[1] Material in this interview is reported in "Fitzgeralds Felt Insecure in France: Now Live Here," *The Baltimore Evening Sun*, 25 October 1932, p. 3.

He spoke enthusiastically of it, as if he considered it one of his best. Of others recently published he was highly critical. With a tinge of surprise in his voice he admitted that "quite a few people seemed to like" one of them—"Babylon Revisited."

Mrs. Fitzgerald also has written successful short stories. Most of them have appeared in *College Humor* and *Scribner's*. Mr. Fitzgerald said he preferred not to make public the title of her novel.

Sitting in his room at the Rennert Hotel he discussed modern literary trends since the day when he left Princeton University to fight with the American Expeditionary Forces[2] and returned to the United States to write *This Side of Paradise*; *Flappers and Philosophers*; *The Beautiful and Damned*; *Tales of the Jazz Age*; *The Vegetable*, a play; *The Great Gatsby*; and *All the Sad Young Men*, a collection of short stories.

"We were a serious generation," he said. "The things I wrote about in *This Side of Paradise* we took as something new, something strange. Last night I attended a fraternity party at the Hopkins. It made me feel old. This generation is lighter than ours. What was new to us is the accepted thing to them."

Mr. Fitzgerald is thirty-five and looks much younger. If his writing has changed measurably in recent years, "as I suppose it has," he has not been aware of it, he said. He spoke with admiration of Ernest Hemingway, William Faulkner, Thornton Wilder, John Dos Passos and others in the new generation of writers whose names were unknown when his novels of flapperdom and other phenomena of the post-war generation were creating a furor.

"No, I can't see that there's been any pronounced political or economic swing in the novel recently," he said. "A few have shown a tendency in that direction, inspired by the depression, but the majority retain their highly individualistic attitude. I think it's a good thing that we're getting over our boom-years period when we pictured life and success as easy, but I think it's a mistake for the novelist to sacrifice his detached viewpoint.

"The American people are just beginning to wake up to the fact that success comes hard. It's been easy in the past. But it's a mistake to think that the increasing concern of novelists with their characters' economic struggles is a new thing in American literature. We had it before the war in Jack London, in Edna Ferber and Fannie Hurst, and in Ida Tarbell with her story of the Standard Oil."[3]

---

[2] Fitzgerald did not go overseas in World War I.

[3] Both Ferber and Hurst were bestselling novelists who wrote about striving heroines; Tarbell was one of the muckrakers who attacked the corruption of big business.

One of the results of the depression is that "young writers just starting out now have only one chance in a hundred of getting a hearing; the publishers not only have cut rates, but also are interested only in big names," Mr. Fitzgerald said.

Seven years ago the Fitzgeralds bade the United States adieu and sailed to make their permanent home in France. Deaths in their families and the depression have brought them back.

"Off there in a little village we had such a horrible feeling of insecurity," Mr. Fitzgerald said. "We had so little information from home, and we kept hearing these reports about business conditions until we didn't know but that any moment the United States would go smash and we'd be cut adrift.

"I'm very much interested in the state of the nation. Personally,—I think it's entirely too big ever to be managed properly. I think it ought to be cut up in six independent political sections. Recently I wired a certain Southern university to hire an economist to work out the six divisions for me, but the university replied that it had no department of economics."

" 'Cellar-Door? Ugh!' " Quoth Baltimore Writers

Baltimore Post / 1932

F. Scott Fitzgerald and most of the rest of Baltimore's authoring tribe think New York writers are way off when they pick such words as "cellar-door" as the most beautiful in the language.

When asked what he thought was the most beautiful word, Fitzgerald promptly replied: "Money." On second thought, however, he said he didn't think that was a particularly witty remark, so he sat down and worked out a list which he "seriously believes" are the ten most beautiful in the English language.

Fitzgerald's choices were: Whip, snap, bumkin, dark, more, wine, ineluctable, pale, Garbo, and clandestine.

Three poets who were questioned as to their preferences agreed that the measure of a word and its associations are far more important in judging the beauty than the mere sound. . . .

Although Baltimore writers showed wide disagreement in their preferences, none could make out why Hendrik Van Loon and Albert Payson Terhune, in New York, think "cellar-door" should be ranked at the top.

Scott Fitzgerald thought Ring Lardner's selections were "darned good" and thoroughly typical, but he chose none of them for his own list. Lardner's ten began with "gangrene" and ended with "crene," which he interpreted as meaning a person who inhales, but doesn't smoke.

F. Scott Fitzgerald Is Visitor in City; New Book Appears Soon

Daily Progress / 1933

Reprinted from the *Daily Progress* [Charlottesville, Va.], 25 May 1933, p. 1. Copyright © *The Daily Progress*. Reprinted by permission.

F. Scott Fitzgerald, author of books on college life and familiar to thousands of readers of weekly periodicals, stopped at the Monticello Hotel last night on a trip through the valley and the Piedmont section. At the hotel this morning, Mr. Fitzgerald expressed surprise at the architectural beauty of the University, the magnitude that was once Virginia, and the superiority of college buildings here through simplicity and graceful times, over those of Princeton, which he ardently admired.

It was Mr. Fitzgerald's first visit to the University, and he admitted himself charmed with the expression of individualism it represented architecturally. Princetonian buildings, he indicated, were achievements in this country of something which had been already attained abroad. He agreed in principle, he said, with the old line opinion that the "Stanford White stuff" was after all, not essentially architecture of utility, the most perfect examples of which may be found on the Ranges at the college here.

The architecture of the college shows to perfection the impossibility of placing beside the buildings of one era those in the style of another period. Any attempt to modulate the Ranges with more modern buildings would, he added, not only fail to satisfy the ends of utility, but would probably not be more pleasing in any way to the eye.

Speaking of the age in which Jefferson's work here became an actuality, Fitzgerald said the eighteenth century's closing marked the end of the period during which it was possible for men to contain in themselves all the wisdom of the centuries. It is impossible, since the death of Goethe, the last of the intellectual giants of this sort, to think of this any longer, he said.

The University community should be proud, Mr. Fitzgerald explained, to know that of the two men who belonged to the eighteenth century who left permanent institutions of learning, Jefferson was one; the other of course, being Benjamin Franklin.

Mr. Fitzgerald also spoke briefly on the topic of the Negro problem in the economic recovery so much discussed in this day of the communistic set-up, especially in the South, and of the right of many thousands of people in other states to be able to say even now that they were once, through colonial boundaries, native Virginians.

A new book, to make its appearance within two or three months and on which he has been at work for six years, was also mentioned by the author. It is understood the trip now being taken by him is in preparation for a final attack upon its last few chapters.

Holds "Flappers" Fail as Parents

New York Times / 1933

The twelve-year-old daughter of F. Scott Fitzgerald, whose novel *This Side of Paradise* dealt with the American flapper some years ago, thinks that most of the girls and boys about whom her father wrote are rather incompetent parents today.

Mr. Fitzgerald is inclined to agree with that opinion.

"Maybe I'm getting old-fashioned," he said. "You know the type—old man Fitzgerald telling what's wrong with the world. But in most sections of the country my crowd aren't doing so well in the mother and father role."

"They don't seem to think a lot about their children," said Frances Scott Fitzgerald, the daughter. "They think the kids are going to be taught everything at school."

"Exactly," put in Fitzgerald. "They sit on their fat hams and leave their own jobs to teachers."

"How about the fathers?" Frances was asked.

"They don't see them very often, except when they come home from business and say go upstairs and be quiet or run around to the other side of the house to play."

"Do children your age respect their parents?"

"Oh, yes, they respect them, I guess. It's just that they don't know them so well. The parents are interested in their children, I think, but—well, they seem to want to do something for them and don't know how."

"I think one thing she was driving at," said the author later, "is that my contemporaries have found their own lack of religious and moral convictions makes them incompetent to train their children."

Perched on the rail of the porch surrounding his rambling old country home, near Baltimore, the novelist continued:

"On the whole, the flappers turned out better than the boys of their age. They are the ones who just missed the war but blame everything that's wrong with them on the war. It's an unhappy generation."

"Right now Zelda (Mrs. Fitzgerald) and I are more interested in the next crop of prom girls than in those of today, or of our day. They are the kids with ex-flappers for mothers and they are having pretty sorry treatment over most of this country. Their mothers will let them do anything just so long as it does not interfere with their own pleasures.

"Perhaps in the morning they'll give some attention to the children, but that afternoon they'll hunch themselves over a bridge table and pack the kids off to the movies where they'll get a two-hour dose of the 'Sins of Susie.'"

Looking at Youth
Mary Margaret McBride / 1934

Reprinted from the *New York World-Telegram,* 4 June 1934, p. 21.
Copyright © *New York World Telegram.* Reprinted by permission.

From school and college these days stream thousands of young Americans to whom the grown-ups should be introduced. . . . In a series of six articles there is presented an unbiased, broad mixture of the startlingly different Young Generation that has come recently into being. . . . Today, in the first article, you learn about young folk of the immediate yesterday and the changed today.

"The young of today have no faith in their parents," mused F. Scott Fitzgerald. "In fact, they obviously consider their fathers and mothers pitiably lacking in common sense—just poor old back numbers who must be petted and babied and endured!"

"You are right," composedly spoke up Miss Frances Scott Fitzgerald from the other side of the room. "We don't think our parents know much about the world. You know why? Well, it's because of the way they act and the things they tell us we ought to do!"

Mr. Fitzgerald and his pretty blonde schoolgirl daughter, known to her intimates as Scottie, agree about the way youth today acts but are not quite of one mind as to the propriety thereof.

It was Scott Fitzgerald, you remember, who practically invented the younger generation a decade and a half ago. He did it with a book called *This Side of Paradise* which produced such a stir that the nation has been in a dither ever since over what youth thinks and feels and means to do with itself.

In the meantime, the author has acquired a younger generation of his own—which naturally makes his interest a bit less academic than it was.

"My daughter's generation spends most of its time looking at itself in its several mirrors and figuring out how to be like Garbo," he commented.

Scottie accepted the challenge with a toss of her yellow bobbed head.

"Well, and if we do?" she countered. "Surely it's a good thing for us to want to make the best of ourselves. We don't really look into mirrors all the time, though. We haven't time. We're too busy reflecting what life is all about. We have to decide these matters for ourselves since our parents don't understand our problems!"

The girl turned her deep blue eyes gravely in my direction.

"Daddy is a fine writer," she confided, exactly as if he had not been in the room. "But as for knowing about life, he doesn't. He's just a child. He hasn't the vaguest idea what is going on today. He knows only things that happened a long time ago—oh, ten, maybe twenty years ago!"

"My generation is not really being brought up by its parents," Scottie startlingly asserted.

"A girl knows well enough it's the bunk if her parents tell her one thing and then do the opposite. Can you blame her? We've learned to use our minds!"

"What is your ambition, Scottie?" inquired her father amiably.

"I want to design scenery and produce shows," she retorted crisply. "I want to have a great deal of money and to make it all myself. But I'll probably marry, too."

When his daughter had departed to put a few licks on her next day's French lesson, her father smiled, and nodded.

"You see? That is what her generation is really like—fond of its parents but completely unimpressed by them; ambitious, poised, cock-sure that it can get whatever it wants; emancipated from the old saws."

In short, Scottie and her contemporaries are the cumulative result of what has happened since Scottie's father set the world by the ears with his talk of the younger generation.

"In 1915," he says, "they didn't yet know what it was all about. They were still almost Victorian, with only here and there a young man or a young woman beginning to suspect that a lot of it until-then sacred beliefs were only bunk and junk. Then 1917 saw the real beginning of dissatisfaction with the existing order. Then the war came along and knocked both men and girls sidewise.

"About 1922, you got the flapper and her boy friend. These young things were created by public opinion and they did their best to live up to what was expected of them. The girls wore their skirts as short as they could get them and any excess of behavior was considered smart. In 1924 came a sharp reaction which took the form with the oncoming generation of condemning the older brothers and sisters. Dresses got sinisterly longer, morals stricter.

"By 1929 these rather priggish young people had given place to a genera-tion with a curious kind of confidence that there's now no word for, a generation that had the world by the tail, never dreaming there would be an end to the good things that came their way. Then the end came and you saw a sickening look of fear and puzzlement grow in girls' eyes.

"By 1933, boys and girls were being more wisely brought out into life. These youngsters know more than any generation ever did, but of course they think they know more even than they do. The only way to handle them is to let life deal with them. I have a feeling they are going to make out better than any of us who have gone before, at that."

F. Scott Fitzgerald Staying at Hotel Here[1]

Asheville Citizen / 1935

Reprinted from the *Asheville Citizen* [Asheville, N.C.], 21 July 1935, pp. 1–2. Copyright 1935, Asheville, N.C. *Citizen-Times*. Reprinted with permission.

The three greatest literary "talents" coming to the front in America so far in the 1930s have been three Southerners—Thomas Wolfe, of Asheville; William Faulkner, of Mississippi; and Erskine Caldwell, of Georgia—in the opinion of F. Scott Fitzgerald, noted author visiting Asheville.

Mr. Fitzgerald, novelist and short story writer, came here several weeks ago. He is a guest at Grove Park Inn.

One of America's most widely read writers of the present day, he yesterday discussed trends in literature in one of his few interviews in many years.

The quality of the American novel has fallen off during the last five years, according to this distinguished vacationist, mustached, affable, very likable. He also finds that writing on the whole was better during the 1920s than it has been so far during the 1930s.

This can be explained in part by the depression, said the deep-thinking Mr. Fitzgerald. "In time of turbulence it (writing) is not usually as good." Poetry and fiction are best written in tranquil times.

"We must remember that there are two kinds of tranquillity, too. One is genuine; the other is the sort that comes when we have finished a task and are utterly worn out, and is not genuine tranquillity.

"In times of turbulence everything, including writing, comes too quickly, too hastily, and this isn't productive of the best literature. On the other hand, the times immediately after turbulence sometimes produce a great flowering of literature."

Illustrating from the period in history known as the Renaissance, the well-known author said: "We can illustrate from the Renaissance. During the time

[1] This interview was substantially repeated in Ed G. Thomas, "Our 'Oh, Yeah' Generation," *Atlanta Journal*, 25 August 1935, magazine section, p. 8. The two interviews may have been the work of the same reporter.

of trouble, there was no flowering by writers and painters. Then followed good work.

"During the time of turbulence, the main thing is to live.

"Therefore as more genuinely tranquil times come, we may expect more in the way of good literature," said Mr. Fitzgerald, who believes that the South's lead in new literary talent so far in the 1930s probably indicates that Dixie has led in the emergence from the depression.

Author Fitzgerald, not yet forty, came into his own as a nationally known writer fifteen years ago with *This Side of Paradise*, which he wrote while in the United States army during the world war.

A member of the Authors' League of America, his writings also include *Flappers and Philosophers, The Beautiful and Damned, Tales of the Jazz Age, The Great Gatsby, All the Sad Young Men, Doctor Diver's Holiday*,[2] *Tender Is the Night*, and *Taps at Reveille*. The latter two have been published within the last year.

In addition he has written scores of short stories for magazines, including sixty-five published in the *Saturday Evening Post* alone.

His latest published work was a short story, "Zone of Accident," which appeared in the *Saturday Evening Post* for last week.

"There's a history behind 'Zone of Accident,'" the writer said.

Three years ago he was taken to Johns Hopkins Hospital, in Baltimore, Md., where he maintains his legal residence, with a case of intestinal influenza.

"I began to consider those weeks just two weeks wasted. I was observant of things going on in the hospital, however, and realized after I left the place that I had been accumulating material for some writing and hadn't known it at the time. So followed 'Intern,' a short story with a hospital as its scene."

Mr. Fitzgerald then decided he wanted to write more of hospitals, medicos, and nurses.

For fifteen consecutive nights he went to the accident room of the Baltimore institution to gather material for more such work. He stayed hours at a time. But the accident cases he had hoped to learn from didn't come in. "The wrecks and emergency cases always occurred just after I had left."

At any rate, he wrote "Zone of Accident," disliked it and cast it aside. Recently he dug it up, rewrote it, and the *Saturday Evening Post* printed it last week.

---

[2] "Dr. Diver's Holiday" was a rejected title for *Tender Is the Night*.

Mr. Fitzgerald's work, largely about young people, has been much read by young people. "This generation of youth has lost faith in its elders unusually early," he lamentingly observed.

"Young people now have a negative philosophy, which they get from uncertainty of their elders and of the times. They are not at the moment idealists. Too much has happened. They have been preached to, lied to. Most generations grow up with idealism, but the expression, 'Oh! Yeah!' comes closer to expressing the feeling of the present younger generation than anything else. They are, like all mankind, essentially spiritual, but just simply haven't found leadership that they can honestly accept."

Asked if he thought young people now prefer any special kind of literature, he said: "I have a thirteen-year-old daughter, Frances. I know things she doesn't like, codes of which she doesn't approve, but it's hard to learn what she likes. Even in the very young I find utter disillusionment. Here one finds the negative philosophy being expressed."

Mr. Fitzgerald, Princeton University graduate, has done some writing since coming to Asheville, but chose not to talk of it. A prominent member of the summer colony at Grove Park Inn, he expects to be here about a month longer.

Fitzgerald's Six Generations

Anthony Buttitta / 1935

Reprinted from the *News and Observer* [Raleigh, N.C.], 1 September 1935, p. 3.[1] Copyright © *News and Observer.* Reprinted by permission.

Six generations have passed in review since 1914, F. Scott Fitzgerald, one of America's most brilliant and distinctive novelists, declared here today in an exclusive interview at the Grove Park Inn where for the past two months he has been working on his new novel which will be released by Scribner's sometime in 1936.[2]

The subject of generations, and the influence of one generation upon another, has always fascinated Mr. Fitzgerald. This interest was definitely noticed in his last work. *Taps at Reveille*, a collection of short stories, including two youth studies "Basil" and "Josephine." His latest novel, *Tender Is the Night*, was well received by both the reading public and the critics.

The six generations as listed and analysed by Mr. Fitzgerald are: Pre-War, the War, Post-War, Boom, Shock and Hard-Times. It is interesting to note that he builds the first three around the war and its effects, and the last three around the rise and fall of our contemporary economic and financial structure.

Mr. Fitzgerald said that the Pre-War generation was one full of inhibitions. It was attached strongly to the Victorian tradition and manner of living. In spite of fancying themselves modern, those of the Pre-War period were fundamentally moral in both ideas and actions. The novel which represents this era and its thought is H. G. Wells's *Anna Veronica*.[3]

Enough has been said of the War generation, according to Mr. Fitzgerald, but the best that has been said about it was Ernest Hemingway's remark "that the words *duty, honor, and courage* lost all reality, and only somethings

---

[1] Buttitta was operating a bookshop in Asheville when he met Fitzgerald. He subsequently exaggerated the extent of their friendship in *After the Good Gay Times* (New York: Viking, 1974).

[2] Following *Tender Is the Night* in 1934, Fitzgerald did not publish another novel in his lifetime.

[3] The title is *Ann Veronica*.

which seemed to have any dignity were names of places, streams and rivers."
This was true first of men and eventually was also true of women. Hemingway
has pictured this "lost" generation in *Farewell to Arms*.

The Post-War generation is an utterly disrupted one. Youth suffered with
interrupted educations. Mr. Fitzgerald finds this generation essentially weak,
and much inclined to be looking to the two older groups for guidance, without
being certain of which to follow as a standard. There is no vitality in this
group, and it is best described in fiction by books like *The Plastic Age* and
Flaming Youth.[4]

Many years are included in the Boom era. The members of this generation,
according to the novelist, "are brassy, metalic and in their ethics unsympa-
thetic. Their best quality is a scorn of weakness, and their worst quality is a
sort of inhumanity." They do not hold their heads as high as they used to,
for their action has been conditioned by parental optimists who once boomed
forth "Maybe in five years, I'll own—the company!" Peter Arno's *Hulla-
ballo*[5] typifies this generation for Mr. Fitzgerald.

The Shock generation is that of the war repeated. It has the same qualities
and is a generation of daring. It is prematurely old, too. The youth of this
generation could not live without an education. It is not a happy one, but will
prove itself more worthy of respect than the two generations which preceded
it. The Shock group is not unlike the generation which grew up under defeat
in the South after the Civil War. The blow gave it dignity. William Faulkner's
Pylon is a somewhat morbid representation of the spirit of the Shock era.

The youngest generation is that of Hard-Times. "The less the parents of
today try to tell their children, the more effective they can be in making them
believe in a few old truths," Mr. Fitzgerald declared emphatically. "This
generation should be held close to whatever elements of character we have
been able to find and develop in ourselves." Mr. Fitzgerald says the book of
this period has yet to be written.

Mr. Fitzgerald was born in St. Paul, Minnesota in 1896, and has always
been writing. He was named after the author of the "Star Spangled Banner"—Francis Scott Key. While attending St. Paul Academy, he wrote in
the backs of his class books. To turn his mind to study, his parents sent him
to the Newman School in New Jersey. Here he started writing musical
comedies.

---

[4] Twenties novels by Percy Marks and Samuel Hopkins Adams about the dissipations
of youth.

[5] *Hullabaloo* (1930) was an illustrated book by Arno.

At Princeton, he wrote an operetta for the Triangle Club. In doing this he failed in algebra, trigonometry, coordinate geometry, and chemistry. The Club produced his show and Fitzgerald played the part of a chorus girl in it. In spite of his thirty-eight years, he is a youthful looking fellow. He has the cosmopolitanism and the finesse of some of his best characters—in fact, he could step out of his own books.

In 1917, he left college to join the army, but did not get to go overseas. It was in the army, however, that he wrote his first novel. "Every Saturday at 1 o'clock when the week was over, I hurried up to the Officers' Club, and there in a room full of smoke, conversation and rattling newspapers, I wrote a 120,000 word novel in the consecutive weekends of three months."

Many publishers called this book, "The Romantic Egotist," the most original manuscript they had received for years—but they would not publish it. Seven New York city editors turned him down flat on a reportial job, and he turned to advertising—the kind that has a nook in trolly-cars. He then sold a few sketches, but gave up his job and returned to his St. Paul home.

He got down to a serious novel and did it. The novel was *This Side of Paradise* which was published in 1920. This work was the bestseller of the period. Two books of short stories followed in rapid succession, *Flappers and Philosophers* (1920) and *Tales of the Jazz Age* (1922). The same year saw the publication of *The Beautiful and Damned* which brought the youthful novelist more serious attention from the critics.

Three years later he completed *The Great Gatsby*. Though most of the material was collected for this work while he was living in post-war Long Island, he wrote it in Rome and on the Riviera. Another book of short stories followed, *All the Sad Young Men*. Last year he wrote a novel of American sophisticates abroad, diagnosing them with keen brilliance, entitled *Tender Is the Night*. A dramatization of this novel will be presented on Broadway this season.[6]

---

[6] No dramatization of *Tender Is the Night* was produced in 1935.

The Other Side of Paradise: Scott Fitzgerald, 40, Engulfed in Despair

Michel Mok / 1936

Long ago, when he was young, cock-sure, drunk with sudden success, F. Scott Fitzgerald told a newspaper man that no one should live beyond thirty.

That was in 1921, shortly after his first novel, *This Side of Paradise*, had burst into the literary heavens like a flowering Roman candle.

The poet-prophet of the post-war neurotics observed his fortieth birthday yesterday in his bedroom of the Grove Park Inn here. He spent the day as he spends all his days—trying to come back from the other side of Paradise, the hell of despondency in which he has writhed for the last couple of years.

He had no company except his soft spoken, Southern, maternal and indulgent nurse and this reporter. With the girl he bantered in conventional nurse-and-patient fashion. With his visitor he chatted bravely, as an actor, consumed with fear that his name will never be in lights again, discusses his next starring role.

He kidded no one. There obviously was as little hope in his heart as there was sunshine in the dripping skies, covered with clouds that veiled the view of Sunset Mountain.

Physically he was suffering the aftermath of an accident eight weeks ago, when he broke his right shoulder in a dive from a fifteen-foot springboard.

But whatever pain the fracture might still cause him, it did not account for his jittery jumping off and onto his bed, his restless pacing, his trembling hands, his twitching face with its pitiful expression of a cruelly beaten child.

Nor could it be responsible for his frequent trips to a highboy, in a drawer of which lay a bottle. Each time he poured a drink into the measuring glass on his bedside table, he would look appealingly at the nurse and ask, "Just one ounce?"

---

[1] When this interview was published, Fitzgerald purportedly attempted suicide by taking an overdose of morphine.

Each time the nurse cast down her eyes without replying.

Fitzgerald, for that matter, did not attempt to make his injury an excuse for his thirst.

"A series of things happened to papa," he said, with mock brightness. "So papa got depressed and started drinking a little."

What the "things" were he refused to explain.

"One blow after another," he said, "and finally something snapped."

Before coming to North Carolina, however, his visitor had learned something of Fitzgerald's recent history from friends in Baltimore, where he lived until last July.

The author's wife, Zelda, had been ill for some years. There was talk, said his friends, of an attempt at suicide on her part one evening when the couple were taking a walk in the country outside Baltimore. Mrs. Fitzgerald, so the story went, threw herself on the tracks before an oncoming express train. Fitzgerald, himself in poor health, rushed after her and narrowly saved her life.

There were other difficulties. Mrs. Fitzgerald finally was taken to a sanitarium near this city, and her husband soon followed her, taking a room in the rock-built Grove Park Inn, one of the largest and most famous resort hotels in America.

But the causes of Fitzgerald's breakdown are of less importance than its effects on the writer. In a piece entitled "Pasting It Together," one of three autobiographical articles published in *Esquire*, which appeared in the March issue of that magazine, Fitzgerald described himself as "a cracked plate."

"Sometimes, though," he wrote, "the cracked plate has to be retained in the pantry, has to be kept in service as a household necessity.

"It can never again be warmed on the stove nor shuffled with the other plates in the dishpan; it will not be brought out for company, but it will do to hold crackers late at night or to go into the ice box under the leftovers.

"Now the standard cure for one who is sunk is to consider those in actual destitution or physical suffering—this is an all-weather beatitude for gloom in general and fairly salutory daytime advice for every one. But at 3 o'clock in the morning . . . the cure doesn't work—and in a real dark night of the soul it is always 3 o'clock in the morning, day after day. At that hour the tendency is to refuse to face things as long as possible by retiring into an infantile dream—but one is continually startled out of this by various conflicts with the world.

"One meets these occasions as quickly and carelessly as possible and retires once more back into the dream, hoping that things will adjust themselves by some great material or spiritual bonanza. But as the withdrawal persists there is less and less chance of the bonanza—one is not waiting for the fade-out of a single sorrow, but rather being an unwilling witness of an execution, the disintegration of one's own personality. . . ."

Yesterday, toward the end of a long, rambling, disjointed talk, he put it in different words, not nearly as poetic but no less moving for that reason:

"A writer like me," he said, "must have an utter confidence, an utter faith in his star. It's an almost mystical feeling, a feeling of nothing-can-happen-to-me, nothing-can-harm-me, nothing-can-touch-me.

"Thomas Wolfe has it. Ernest Hemingway has it. I once had it. But through a series of blows, many of them my own fault, something happened to that sense of immunity and I lost my grip."

In illustration, he told a story about his father:

"As a boy, my father lived in Montgomery County, Maryland. Our family has been mixed up quite a bit in American history. My great-grandfather's brother was Francis Scott Key, who wrote 'The Star-Spangled Banner'; I was named for him. My father's aunt was Mrs. Suratt, who was hanged after the assassination of Lincoln because Booth had planned the deed in her house—you remember that three men and a woman were executed.

"As a youngster of nine, my father rowed spies across the river. When he was twelve he felt that life was finished for him. As soon as he could, he went West, as far away from the scenes of the Civil War as possible. He started a wicker-furniture factory in St. Paul. A financial panic in the nineties struck him and he failed.

"We came back East and my father got a job as a soap salesman in Buffalo. He worked at this for some years. One afternoon—I was ten or eleven—the phone rang and my mother answered it. I didn't understand what she said but I felt that disaster had come to us. My mother, a little while before, had given me a quarter to go swimming. I gave the money back to her. I knew something terrible had happened and I thought she could not spare the money now.

"Then I began to pray. 'Dear God,' I prayed, 'please don't let us go to the poorhouse; please don't let us go to the poorhouse.' A little while later my father came home. I had been right. He had lost his job.

"That morning he had gone out a comparatively young man, a man full of strength, full of confidence. He came home that evening, an old man, a completely broken man. He had lost his essential drive, his immaculateness of purpose. He was a failure the rest of his days."

Fitzgerald rubbed his eyes, his mouth, quickly walked up and down the room.

"Oh," he said, "I remember something else. I remember that when my father came home my mother said to me, 'Scott, say something to your father.'

"I didn't know what to say. I went up to him and asked, 'Father, who do you think will be the next President?'" He looked out of the window. He didn't move a muscle. Then he said: 'I think Taft will.'

"My father lost his grip and I lost my grip. But now I'm trying to get back. I started by writing those pieces for *Esquire*. Perhaps they were a mistake. Too much de profundis. My best friend, a great American writer—he's the man I call my artistic conscience in one of the *Esquire* articles—wrote me a furious letter. He said I was stupid to write that gloomy personal stuff."

"What are your plans at the moment, Mr. Fitzgerald? What are you working on now?"

"Oh, all sorts of things. But let's not talk about plans. When you talk about plans, you take something away from them."

Fitzgerald left the room.

"Despair, despair, despair," said the nurse. "Despair day and night. Try not to talk about his work or his future. He does work, but only very little— maybe three, four hours a week."

Soon he returned. "We must celebrate the author's birthday," he said gayly. "We must kill the fatted calf or, at any rate, cut the candled cake."

He took another drink. "Much against your better judgment, my dear," he smiled at the girl.

Heeding the nurse's advice, the visitor turned the talk to the writer's early days and Fitzgerald told how *This Side of Paradise* came to be written.

"I wrote it when I was in the army," he said. "I was nineteen. I rewrote the whole book a year later. The title was changed, too. Originally, it was called 'The Romantic Egotist.'"

"Isn't *This Side of Paradise* a beautiful title? I'm good at titles, you know. I've published four novels and four volumes of short-stories. All my novels have good titles—*The Great Gatsby, The Beautiful and Damned*, and *Tender Is the Night*. That's my latest book. I worked on it four years.

"Yes, I wrote *This Side of Paradise* in the army. I didn't go overseas—my army experience consisted mostly of falling in love with a girl in each city I happened to be in.

"I almost actually went across. They actually marched us onto a transport and then marched us right off again. Influenza epidemic or something. That was about a week before the armistice.

"We were quartered at Camp Mills, in Long Island. I sneaked out of bounds into New York—there was a girl concerned, no doubt—and I missed the train back to Camp Sheridan, Ala., where we had been trained.

"So this is what I did. Went to the Pennsylvania station and commandeered an engine and a cab to take me to Washington to join the troops. I told the railroad people I had confidential war papers for President Wilson. Couldn't wait a minute. Couldn't be intrusted to the mails. They fell for my bluff. I'm sure it's the only time in the history of the United States Army that a lieutenant has commandeered a locomotive. I caught up with the regiment in Washington. No, I wasn't punished."

"But how about *This Side of Paradise*?"

"That's right—I'm wandering. After we were mustered out I went to New York. Scribners turned my book down. Then I tried to get a job on a newspaper. I went to every newspaper office with the scores and lyrics of the Triangle shows of the two or three previous years under my arm—I had been one of the big boys in the Triangle Club at Princeton and I thought that would help. The office boys were not impressed."

One day, Fitzgerald ran into an advertising man who told him to stay away from the newspaper business. He helped him to get a job with the Barron Collier agency, and for some months Fitzgerald wrote slogans for street car cards.

"I remember," he said, "the hit I made with a slogan I wrote for the Muscatine Steam Laundry in Muscatine, Iowa—'We keep you clean in Muscatine.' I got a raise for that. 'It's perhaps a bit imaginative,' said the boss, 'but still it's plain that there's a future for you in this business. Pretty soon this office won't be big enough to hold you.'"

And so it turned out. It didn't take Fitzgerald long to get bored to the point of pain, and he quit. He went to St. Paul, where his parents again were living, and proposed that his mother give him the third floor of her home for a while and keep him in cigarettes.

"She did, and there in three months I completely rewrote my book. Scribners took the revised manuscript in 1919, and they brought it out in the spring of 1920."

In *This Side of Paradise*, Fitzgerald had one of his principal characters take a crack at the popular authors of the period—some of whom are popular still—in these words:

"Fifty thousand dollars a year! My God, look at them, look at them—Edna Ferber, Gouverneur Morris, Fannie Hurst, Mary Roberts Rinehart—not producing among 'em one story or novel that will last ten years. This man Cobb—I don't think he's either clever or amusing—and what's more, I don't think many people do, except the editors. He's just groggy with advertising. And—oh, Harold Bell Wright and Zane Grey, Ernest Poole and Dorothy Canfield try, but they are hindered by their absolute lack of any sense of humor."

And the lad wound up by saying it was no wonder that such English writers as Wells, Conrad, Galsworthy, Shaw, and Bennett depended on America for over half their sales.

What does Fitzgerald think of the literary situation in this country today?

"It has improved a lot," he said. "The whole thing broke with *Main Street.* Ernest Hemingway, I think, is the greatest living writer of English. He took that place when Kipling died. Next comes Thomas Wolfe and then Faulkner and Dos Passos.

"Erskine Caldwell and a few others have come up just a bit after our generation, and they haven't done quite so well. We were products of prosperity. The best art is produced in times of riches. The men who came some years after us didn't have the chance we had."

Has he changed his mind on questions of economics? Amory Blaine, the hero of *This Side of Paradise,* predicted the success of the Bolshevik experiment in Russia, foresaw eventual government ownership of all industries in this country.

"Oh, but I made an awful boner," said Fitzgerald. "Do you remember I said publicity would destroy Lenin? That was a fine prophecy. He became a saint.

"My views? Well, in a pinch, they'd still be pretty much toward the left."

Then the reporter asked him how he felt now about the jazz-mad, gin-mad generation whose feverish doings he chronicled in *This Side of Paradise.* How had they done? How did they stand up in the world?

"Why should I bother myself about them?" he asked. "Haven't I enough worries of my own? You know as well as I do what has happened to them.

"Some became brokers and threw themselves out of windows. Others became bankers and shot themselves. Still others became newspaper reporters. And a few became successful authors."

His face twitched.

"Successful authors!" he cried. "Oh, my God, successful authors!"

He stumbled over to the highboy and poured himself another drink.

Wanger Blends Abruptness with Charm in Personality[1]

John D. Hess / 1939

The public personality of Walter Wanger '15 is a disturbing blend of abruptness and charm. At this particular interview he sat quietly in a chair exuding power and authority in easy breaths, seemingly indifferent to anything I said, but quickly, suddenly, sharply catching a phrase, questioning it, commenting upon it, grinding it into me, smiling, and then apparently forgetting all about me again.

In a chair directly across from Mr. Wanger was Mr. F. Scott Fitzgerald, who looked and talked as if he had long since become tired of being known as the spokesman of that unfortunate lost generation of the 1920s. Mr. Fitzgerald is working on the script of Mr. Wanger's picture, *Winter Carnival.*

Both men were graciously sincere. Both men were distinct and well-spoken in their ideas, of which there were enough to supply a college newspaper with editorials for six weeks. Any thought of Hollywood jargon was an absurdity.

Both men agreed that Dartmouth '39, Dartmouth '40 and all their contemporaries were a part of a generation that looks different, thinks different, acts different than their own. Both men agreed, significantly, that their own generation had as its goal and god unlovely, big-medicine totem pole of Success. And both felt that this new generation, smashed by a giant depression, battered by half a dozen different world ideologies, was living with a chip on its shoulder, but not asking to scratch and battle for Success only. This generation, they said is working and fighting toward a bigger, brighter goal which might include security, independence, democracy, or any other non-material ideal.

[1] This article in the Dartmouth College newspaper was written when Fitzgerald was in Hanover, New Hampshire, with the location crew for the *Winter Carnival* movie. It is based on his last interview, but Fitzgerald is not quoted; producer Wanger was the more important figure for the reporter. Fitzgerald, who was writing the screenplay with Budd Schulberg, was fired for getting drunk at Dartmouth. Schulberg later incorporated these events and a fictionalized portrait of Fitzgerald into his 1950 novel *The Disenchanted.*

Mr. Fitzgerald and Mr. Wanger had political differences, but each insisted that today's youth was more humanity-minded, more social-minded, more life-and-not-money-minded than their own generation had been.

At the end of half an hour Mr. Wanger, the Myth, had become Mr. Wanger, the Reality—a transition of no little accomplishment even for a movie man.

Index